X-PLANES 17

McDONNELL XP-67 "MOONBAT"

Steve Richardson and Peggy Mason

SERIES EDITOR TONY HOLMES

OSPREY
PUBLISHING

OSPREY PUBLISHING

Bloomsbury Publishing Plc

Kemp House, Chawley Park, Cumnor Hill, Oxford, OX2 9PH, UK

29 Earlsfort Terrace, Dublin 2, Ireland

1385 Broadway, 5th Floor, New York, NY 10018, USA

Email; info@ospreypublishing.com

www.ospreypublishing.com

OSPREY is a trademark of Osprey Publishing Ltd

First published in Great Britain in 2022

© Osprey Publishing Ltd, 2022

A catalog record for this book is available from the British Library.

ISBN: PB: 9781472853035; eBook 9781472853004;
ePDF 9781472853028; XML 9781472853011

22 23 24 25 26   10 9 8 7 6 5 4 3 2 1

Artwork by Adam Tooby

Index by Fionbar Lyons

Typeset by PDQ Digital Media Solutions, Bungay, UK

Printed and bound in India by Replika Press Private Ltd.

MIX
Paper from
responsible sources
FSC® C016779

Osprey Publishing supports the Woodland Trust, the UK's leading woodland
conservation charity.

To find out more about our authors and books visit www.ospreypublishing.com.
Here you will find extracts, author interviews, details of forthcoming events and
the option to sign up for our newsletter.

Acknowledgments

Many people and organizations have
provided us with material that we
previously had no idea even existed.
Special thanks to Mark Nankivil,
President of the Greater St Louis Air and
Space Museum, for sharing photos and
drawings from the museum's collection
and also from the vast collection of
Gerald Balzer, whose name will be
familiar to aviation historians for his many
articles and books on vintage aircraft.
Another source of unique materials was
Ron Farver, son of Lyle Farver, who we
believe was the originator of the highly
blended surface configuration at both
Glenn L. Martin and then McDonnell
Aircraft. Kimble McCutcheon of the
Aircraft Engine Historical Society provided
a wealth of information on the Continental
I-1430 as well as an education in aircraft
superchargers and turbochargers. And of
course our editor at Osprey Publishing,
Tom Milner, for helping guide us through
the entire complex process of creating a
book and its illustrations. These, and so
many more, made this book possible with
their generosity and knowledge.
Thanks to all!

Front Cover

January 6, 1944. With a crowd of
McDonnell Aircraft and USAAF people
watching from the ground, including
James S. McDonnell himself, the sole
XP-67 prototype makes its first flight
over Scott Field across the Mississippi
River from St Louis. The flight had to be
cut short because of overheating in both
engines' turbosupercharger
compartments, due to a design problem
with the ductwork and not, as generally
stated, fires in the engines themselves.
(Cover artwork by Adam Tooby)

Previous Page

Summer 1944, and the McDonnell
XP-67 sits on the tarmac at Lambert
Airport in St Louis, ready for flight in its
final configuration. (Air Force Museum)

X PLANES

CONTENTS

INTRODUCTION

The 1930s were a time of revolutionary change in military aviation. Biplanes, which had been the mainstream configuration for almost all types of aircraft since the Wright brothers, were finally giving way to monoplanes. Giulio Douhet in Italy, Billy Mitchell in the United States, and Hugh Trenchard in Great Britain had advanced the concept of strategic bombing as a decisive element in future warfighting. So pervasive had the idea become that it formed the basis for Stanley Baldwin's 1932 speech to the British Parliament where he delivered the famous line, "the bomber will always get through." If that were true, and if the results were anything like the predictions of the theorists, strategic bombing of a nation would be catastrophic for its capability to wage war, to say nothing of the prospect of immense civilian casualties. In fact, Harold MacMillan wrote after the war that leaders of the time "thought of air warfare in 1938 rather as people think of nuclear war today."

If bombers posed such a fundamental threat to a nation's security, then clearly some counter to them needed to be found. Fighter/interceptor aircraft were the obvious answer, but in order to be maximally effective they needed to have a long enough range to hit the bombers as far from their targets as possible, and a rapid enough rate of climbing to reach the high altitudes where bombers were expected to be operating to avoid ground-based antiaircraft artillery.

In July 1939, James S. McDonnell left the well-established Glenn L. Martin Company to form a company of his own in St Louis, Missouri. It would ultimately become the largest military aircraft manufacturer in America, producing thousands of legendary fighters for air forces

Above and Right:
The beginning and the end of McDonnell's XP-67. (Gerald Balzer Collection, Greater St Louis Air and Space Museum)

and navies around the world. But where did it all start? What was the spark that lit that fuse? How could a tiny new company compete with, and ultimately triumph over, huge established companies whose names were household words?

It started with innovation and vision, the willingness to push boundaries and explore the possible, far beyond what others were willing to do. McDonnell and his initial small team believed that a radical reshaping of the aircraft itself could pay off in improved performance. Having tried and failed to interest Martin in the concept, they were willing to put their careers on the line and make a fresh start on their own. There were some hard times initially, but ultimately they were successful in getting a contract from the US Army Air Corps (USAAC) to turn their concept into hardware, as the McDonnell XP-67.

Even before the United States entered World War II in December 1941, President Franklin D. Roosevelt was urging the country to increase preparations for war. In his January 1941 State of the Union address, Roosevelt noted, "the immediate need is a swift and driving increase in our armament production." He said, specifically, "We are behind schedule in turning out finished airplanes; we are working day and night to solve the innumerable problems and to catch up." To that end, in October 1941, McDonnell's relatively new company joined other manufacturers in designing and building aircraft to strengthen the military's air arms.

It is as well to point out up front that the name "Moonbat," which has come to be universally attached to the aircraft, was never mentioned at the time. Apart from its designation of XP-67, the only other identifier that was ever officially applied to the aircraft was its classified project number, MX-127. In keeping with popular tradition, however, the "Moonbat" moniker has been retained for this book's title but will not be used in the text. The aircraft actually picked up an unofficial nickname from the US Army Air Force (USAAF) pilots who flew it: "Flying Fillet," due to its unique shape. For some reason, that has not stuck in the popular mind, but it is highly descriptive of the startling new look that was unveiled at the aircraft's roll-out in November 1943.

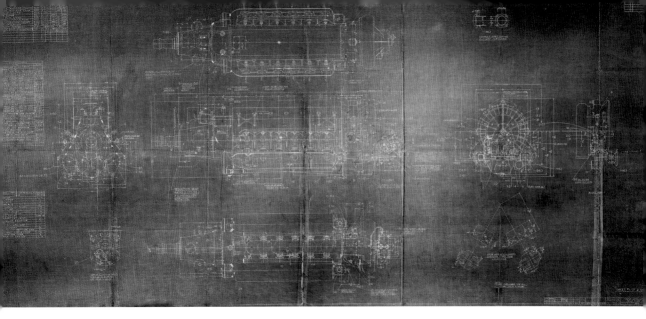

CHAPTER ONE

ORIGINS

On the eve of World War II, the USAAC realized that its latest generation of frontline fighters might be adequate for the current threats they would be facing, but would lack the performance to deal with near- and long-term projected threats. It was apparent that in order to keep pace with developments in Europe in particular, two things were needed: better engines and better airframes to put them in. Each of these produced a "Request for Data" that was actually more of a request for proposals. The first was for engines, around which aircraft could be designed to meet the ambitious requirements spelled out in the second.

Request for Data R40-A, issued on September 11, 1939, was meant to get industry's thoughts on high-power (1,800–2,400hp) engines that were nevertheless compact and lightweight. One goal was to find out whether such engines could be made small enough to be mounted inside the wings of large aircraft such as bombers, but there were three different categories of engines that were of interest.

The USAAC Research Board had given first priority for advanced engine investigations to "specialized power plants to meet the specific requirements of pursuit aviation and the several types of bombardment," also noting that "concentration should be placed on liquid cooled engines of the following types:

1. Flat engines with small frontal area, 1,800 to 2,000 horsepower category.
2. Multi-cylinder, multi-bank engines of circular arrangement and small frontal area, 1,800 to 2400 horsepower category.

XP-67 was literally designed around the Continental I-1430 engine, shown here in its final form. Originally it would have had a two-stage, two-speed supercharger rather than single-stage, single-speed as shown here. (Ron Farver Collection)

3. Inverted Vee types with special military ratings from 1,500 to 1,800 horsepower as **specifically adapted to pursuit airplanes of all types.**" (emphasis added)

The four companies that submitted proposals were Wright, Allison, Continental, and Pratt & Whitney. Allison and Continental each submitted two engines for consideration, Wright and Pratt & Whitney one apiece.

Wright called its engine the R-2160 "Tornado." It was an inline radial engine, consisting of seven banks of six cylinders each. As per the designator, it had 2,160 cubic inches displacement packed into its 96in. length, but was just 35½in. in diameter. Its dry weight was 2,400lb and it was able to produce 2,350hp for takeoff, giving it a power-to-weight ratio of 0.97hp/lb and a specific power of 1.08hp/in^3.

Pratt & Whitney, who have always been strongly associated with air-cooled radial engines, proposed something completely different for R40-A. It was a liquid-cooled H-block engine with 24 cylinders arranged in four blocks of six cylinders each, with two blocks on opposite sides of the engine. Displacement was 2,240 cubic inches initially but later increased to 2,600 cubic inches, yielding 1,800–2,200hp. Unusually, the engine's designation, R-1800, was not based on displacement but on the lower end of the estimated power rating. Like the Wright engine, the R-1800's weight was 2,400lb, but even the upper end of its estimated rating gave it a slightly inferior power-to-weight ratio of 0.92hp/lb but a higher specific power of 1.22hp/in^3.

Allison's two bids were for different versions of its V-3420, a concept it had reluctantly explored several years earlier at the request of the USAAC. The basic engine consisted of two of its V-1710s engines joined to a common crankshaft and fitted with fuel injection instead of carburetion. Considerable development led to its V-3420A variant, which formed the basis of the company's R40-A proposal. Its projected performance capabilities became moot when it was rejected out of hand by the committee due to its size, making it unsuitable for "any but the largest bombardment types. The front view of this engine is essentially the upper half of a circle 60 inches in diameter." The committee concluded that it "does not well fulfill the requirements . . . for installation in pursuit, medium bombardment or other high

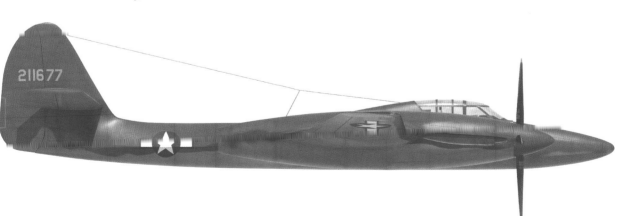

XP-67 roll-out and taxi testing, November–December 1943.

XP-67 first flight, January 6, 1944. Inboard sections of inlets are bulged outward to catch more air. Large topside outlet added to each nacelle, and four smaller ones at mid-nacelle, masked here by wing. Flight test striping has been applied.

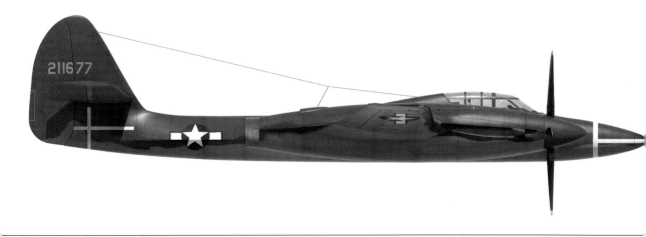

performance military aircraft." Nevertheless, this engine plays a role in the XP-67 story.

Continental's entry was its Model XB-2860, which essentially doubled the company's O-1430, a horizontally opposed engine that it had previously developed but that had been beset by technical issues involving details of cylinder design as well as contractual reimbursement issues with the USAAC. The committee did not favor pursuing this concept because it failed to meet the minimum horsepower requirements and therefore could not be given a Figure of Merit, a top-level factor defined by the committee that could be used to compare all entrants. They were interested, though, in a separate concept, the I-1430, an inverted-vee design with the same displacement as the O-1430 (and therefore, somewhat confusingly, a similar designation). The committee viewed any attempt by Continental to develop both engines as risky. They found the I-1430 "very adaptable for use in small high performance pursuit and interceptor airplanes. In addition, the development of this design would afford the Air Corps a second source of supply for engines in this category." Significantly, "[t]he Committee also found that this design offered possibilities of increased output over that to be expected from the V-1710 engine." Not specifically mentioned in that estimate was weight or size, both of which would later become issues with respect to comparisons between the I-1430 and the V-1710, not to mention license-built V-1650 Merlin engines.[1]

As fallout from R40-A, the I-1430 became a real program. But whose? Brig Gen George H. Brett, Chief of Materiel Division[2] at the time, approved the recommendations of the committee regarding

---

[1]   A note on nomenclature: Continental's engine was referred to by several different designations at the time. I-1430 was a basic designator, with IX-1430 and XI-1430 both using the "X" to emphasize its experimental nature, and IV-1430 standing for Inverted Vee. Where directly quoting contemporary sources, those sources' designations will be retained. Otherwise, the basic I-1430 designation will be used.

[2]   Materiel Division was responsible, through its Engineering Section, for overseeing experimental aircraft and accessories as well as generally keeping informed about advances in technology in order to intelligently formulate programs that could capitalize on those advances for what today would be called "the warfighter." The Engineering Section also initiated contracts with industry to develop and manufacture such items, with an eye toward their standardization for eventual production if warranted.

R40-A results. At the same time, he was also deeply involved with Treasury Secretary Henry Morgenthau's advisory group on aircraft engines, which President Roosevelt had asked Morgenthau to convene because of a problem that was rapidly becoming a crisis.

The USAAC had chosen to use liquid-cooled inline engines in virtually all of its fighter fleet. Its latest aircraft – the P-38, P-39, and P-40 – all used versions of Allison's V-1710. Production of these planes was being dramatically ramped up in accordance with massive USAAC expansion plans generated by President Roosevelt the previous year. More aircraft meant more engines, specifically Allison engines, yet production of V-1710s had virtually collapsed due to technical problems. In the first six months of 1940, Allison was able to produce only 64 V-1710s.

As an example of the effect this was already having, France had ordered a number of H87 (P-40 export variant) aircraft from Curtiss in a desperate attempt to shore up its air defenses. But those aircraft would need country-specific modifications for compatibility with the rest of France's forces, and those changes would have to be trial-fitted and integrated on a few demonstration aircraft. Obtaining just those few trial aircraft proved to be impossible due to the V-1710 shortage. A clearly frustrated Morgenthau summed it up on May 22, 1940: "[W]e are in simply a deplorable condition . . . unless we can get them five engines to try the thing out, their whole program is set back two months . . . you might as well ask me to give you five more Hope diamonds as to give you five Allison engines."

Morgenthau's group explored a number of paths forward, in the event that the Allison problem proved to be unsolvable, and one of them was to directly affect the future XP-67 program. The three main options were to help Allison overcome its largely internal roadblocks, to quickly obtain a license for building the Rolls-Royce Merlin engine in the US (or Canada, although that option quickly disappeared), and to proceed with "the Continental engine," although there seems to have been a bit of confusion at the time over whether the latter meant the flat O-1430 or the inverted-vee I-1430, which then existed only in the form of a single test cylinder engine and plans for making that the basis of a full-featured production engine.

XP-67 after the February–March 1944 rebuild, but before the summer 1944 rework. Inlet ducts and forward nacelle contours have been revised to reduce drag and increase cooling. Rear nacelles have been cut back to expose turbocharger exhausts, and multiple venting inlets and outlets have been added for increased cooling inside nacelles. Propeller blades have been given cuffs. Flight test striping varied throughout this stage of the program.

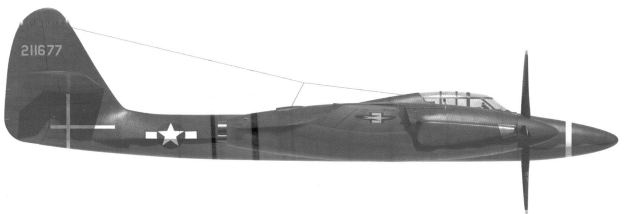

There was, however, deep-seated mistrust within the USAAC, spreading into Morgenthau's committee, of Continental's ability to successfully bring such an engine to production. One of the possibilities that was seriously discussed by Morgenthau's group involved taking their design and giving it to someone else to manufacture. Brig Gen Brett held a remarkable meeting on May 20, 1940, with K. T. Keller, the president of Chrysler, that discussed that subject. A memo documenting that meeting survives. According to it, the meeting began with "a brief summary of the Continental Motors situation outlining the difficulties which would confront Chrysler if the latter attempted to buy it." Also mentioned was "the possibility of building the Rolls-Royce [Merlin] engine," with the comment that "a deal with Rolls-Royce would be very much simpler and would expedite the production of motors . . . General Brett went on to say that the Army had put a great deal of money into financing the development of this Continental motor. Further, that the Continental cylinder when properly developed would be far superior to any now available. It was primarily because of the cylinder design that the Army was so anxious to see someone like Chrysler with its management and engineering ability take hold of that motor and really push it."

The distinction between the "Continental motor" and the "Continental cylinder" is significant. "Motor" generally refers to the flat O-1430 engine mentioned earlier, while "cylinder" means the single engine cylinder that had been built to demonstrate some innovative design features that could be applied to a complete engine. In certain cases, however, it seems that "motor" within the context of those discussions might also mean a future development deriving from that single cylinder. This in fact is what became the I-1430. It seems strange that a single cylinder could be given equal weight by the USAAC with other contractors' fully formed engines, but that was the case.

The meeting took an odd turn when one of the Chrysler attendees asked whether the Continental engine was patented. A memo from Phillip Young, one of Morgenthau's assistants, notes that "General Brett replied that it was not patented but that the Army held the

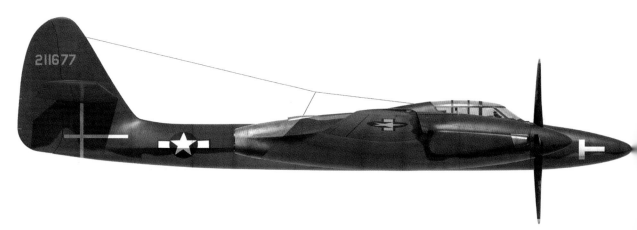

XP-67 final configuration, late summer 1944 to last flight, September 6. Virtually all of the added scoops have been removed to reduce drag. Rear nacelles have been revised again to almost completely enclose turbo exhausts with bare metal panels of revised configuration.

rights." Under further questioning, "the General made the statement that it had never been the practice of the Army to withdraw the manufacture of such a product from the company which had been doing the developmental work." Young concluded by summing up his impression of the meeting: "I see little hope for expediting development of the Continental motor as long as General Brett sticks to his present policy. On the one hand, Continental evidently has not the financial resources, the management ability nor the engineering ability to develop the large Continental motor within a reasonable time; on the other hand, the Army, although it owns the rights to the motor and has financed a large part of the development costs, states that it cannot turn over the job to another manufacturer. If this is truly an emergency and the development of that motor is necessary, more independent money must be put into Continental and adequate management and engineering ability be persuaded to make what looks like an unwise business investment by buying control of Continental, or the Army must set a precedent by withdrawing that motor from Continental and giving it to some one else."

When the dust settled after this apparently contentious session, Continental managed to retain its independent identity and push ahead on its own. Chrysler's attention turned away from acquiring the I-1430 and, under urging by Morgenthau's study group, toward license production of the Rolls-Royce Merlin, although in the end it decided that it would prefer building an engine of its own design. That decision on Chrysler's part led directly to granting the Merlin license to Packard instead.

The inverted-vee engine that Continental produced from it single-cylinder demonstrator was an engineering marvel for the time. Although targeted to equal or exceed the power output of the Allison V-1710, it was much more compact, having a 27 percent smaller frontal area. Less frontal area meant a smaller forward fuselage for a single-engine aircraft or smaller engine nacelles for multi-engine ones, and thus significantly lower drag. Lower drag with equal power was expected to mean higher speeds, especially critical for closing the performance gap between American and European fighters of the early World War II years. A smaller, lighter, more efficient engine needing less fuel to perform its missions meant a smaller, lighter, more efficient aircraft that should consequently be less expensive to manufacture and operate. That was the vision for the I-1430, and when it reached the hardware stage it looked promising indeed.

The engine had 12 cylinders in a 60-degree inverted-vee configuration. Although its designation was "1430," the actual displacement of the pistons was 1,425in^3. The crankcase was an aluminum casting to save weight. A machined steel-forged crankshaft was supported by seven main bearings, made of silver backed by steel. Integrally forged flanges connected the crankshaft to the reduction gear drive at the front and the accessory drive at the rear of the engine. Dome-top pistons with solid skirts were fitted. The rocker arms were forged steel, and one of them would eventually cause fatal trouble for the XP-67. A gear-driven centrifugal supercharger was fitted. Initially

Proposed P-67E photo-reconnaissance variant. Piston engines (Allison V-171 or Rolls-Royce V-1650-11) and jet engines (General Electric I-20) in lengthened nacelles. Raised cockpit with bubble canopy. Cameras mounted in aft fuselage just behind wing trailing edge. No armament.

this was a two-speed device, but by the time the engine was ready for installation in aircraft the second stage had been dropped. An exhaust-driven turbosupercharger (generally shortened to just "turbo" in period documents, although rarely if ever "turbocharger," which appears not to have been in common usage at the time) was also fitted on the only two aircraft to ever fly with the I-1430, the XP-67 and Lockheed's XP-49.

Although technically promising, the I-1430 was still viewed with "approbation" in some quarters. In a November 6, 1941 letter from Brig Gen O. P. Echols, Chief of Materiel Division, to the assistant chief, it was recommended that the program be pushed to an early conclusion. The reason for this was a report from then-Maj Jimmy Doolittle, who would soon gain eternal fame by leading the first bombing raid on the Japanese homeland, that stated "the 1430 is being advanced not at all." Others in the USAAC technical offices were not so gloomy about the engine's prospects. A letter went out on November 18 from Lt Col F. O. Carroll, Chief of Experimental Section at Wright Field, admitting that there were serious problems with the cylinder assembly, but that the rate of progress was actually better than usual, compared with similar programs by other engine manufacturers. That same day, Brig Gen G. C. Kenney sent a response back to Brig Gen Echols, giving his opinion that "the true status of this project lies intermediate between Major Doolittle's pessimistic report and Power Plant Laboratory's optimistic views." There was reason for measured optimism: up to that point, the new Continental product had suffered no failures in its main components, the crankcase, crankshaft, reduction gears, rear accessory section, piston rods, or connecting rods. After this latest challenge, the I-1430 program was again allowed to proceed.

As with the other R40-A engines, the question became: What, exactly, were they needed for? What aircraft needed them in order to meet their required levels of performance? The answer was the second Request for Data: R40-C, for advanced aircraft technologies.

R40-C, issued through the offices of Gen H. H. Arnold, the Chief of the USAAC, was approved and issued on February 20, 1940. It invited a selected list of aircraft manufacturers to submit proposals on their latest designs. The intent was to provide enough information to enable the launch of a three-phase development program during the 1940 fiscal year for experimental single-engine, single-seat pursuit–interceptor aircraft.

The issuing memo to Brig Gen Brett from Materiel Division's Engineering Section describes R40-C as "an effort principally to gain approximately five months on the F.Y. 1941 [1941 fiscal year] experimental pursuit development. It is estimated that, under this proposed Request for Data, approximately 100 different designs will be submitted, ranging all the way from conventional type small airplanes (6,000 lb.) to non-conventional tail first, pusher types indicated around highly experimental engines." These were weird, untried configurations using "highly experimental" engines, but there was still an expectation of quantity production in two years "or sooner." This might have been possible in Germany and Japan, as they proved with the former's "People's Fighter" program (which kicked off in August 1944, with a flying prototype Heinkel He 162 in December 1944) and the latter's "19-shi" specification (issued in July 1944, with a prototype Mitsubishi J8M1 unpowered test flight in January 1945). But such schedule compression was very rare in the American contracting environment with military oversight. True, North American's NA-73 and Lockheed's XP-80 showed that such things were not impossible, but in the former case the requirements and contractual oversight came from the British government, while in the latter case normal processes were set aside to an amazing extent, with the authorizing contract not appearing until four months after design work had begun. The same sense of urgency unfortunately would not arise with experimental aircraft generated by R40-C.

Early in 1939, the USAAC had realized that development of modern pursuit aircraft would be aided if a monetary incentive was offered to manufacturers. On July 17, 1939, $6M ($2.4M in existing Research and Development funding and $3.6M of new money) was set aside to construct single-seat pursuit aircraft in two categories, as initially framed:

- two each of at least three models capable of at least 425mph at "approximately" 15,000ft, to be modifications of existing models. USAAC correspondence in advance of go-ahead on R40-C describes this category as "aircraft to be developed by cleaning up, lightening, and otherwise modifying certain models which have been substantially reduced to practice. Only by following such a method may we expect to get Pursuit aircraft with improved performance for production in Fiscal Year 1941."

- two each of at least two models with a maximum speed of 525mph at the same altitude, to be new designs: "[T]hese aircraft to be entirely of new design, and construction to be started and completed as rapidly as practicable, in order that prototypes may be available for quantity production in Fiscal Year 1942, or sooner."

Proposed P-67C fighter variant. Piston engines (Allison V-1710-119 or Rolls-Royce V-1650-11) and jet engines (General Electric I-20) in lengthened nacelles. Raised cockpit with bubble canopy. Wide range of armament options in nose included baseline 6 x .50cal, 8 x .60cal, 8 x 20mm, 12 x .50cal, or 8 x 37mm.

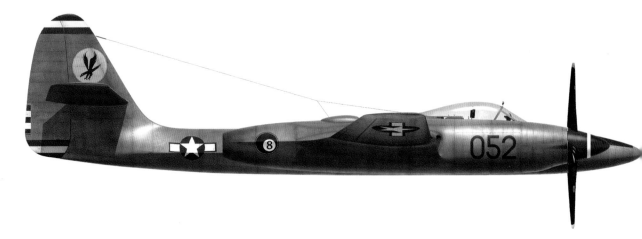

The first experimental article of each would be a flying mock-up with provisions for a pilot and space for military equipment, but not the equipment itself. The second article would be an actual prototype for production; it was to be built concurrently with the first, "but actual delivery will be held in abeyance pending functional tests of the airplane–power plant–propeller combination. Upon satisfactory completion of such tests, the second article will be fully completed with all military equipment in place and will then be tested as an actual prototype for production."

Specific performance goals were formally established as USAAC Type Specification XC-622, issued on November 27, 1939. Request for Data R40-C was then issued on February 1, 1940, and the competition for future advanced aircraft began in earnest. R40-C was initially sent to nine major manufacturers (actually eight, but the St Louis Aircraft Division of Curtiss-Wright was treated as a distinct entity in parallel with the main Curtiss Aircraft Division). Later, four more were added, including the new McDonnell Aircraft Corporation (MAC), also in St Louis, located in a tiny building

REQUIREMENT	MINIMUM	DESIRED	COMMENTS
Takeoff, clear 50ft obstacle, sea level	–	3,000ft	Operations from sod field 3,000ft long
Time to climb to 20,000ft	5.0 min	7.0 min (max)	Military power for 5 minutes, then normal for remainder of time
Maximum speed	425mph	525mph	Military power, 20,000ft
	360mph	460mph	Military power, 5,000ft
Endurance at 20,000ft	1.5hr	1.5hr	
Landing, clear 50ft obstacle, stop with brakes	–	3,000ft	Operations from sod field 3,000ft long
Armament	4 guns (.30-cal, .50-cal, 20mm, 37mm options)		

Main R40-C (Specification XC-622) fighter performance goals, gleaned from a number of aircraft reports and publications. "Minimum" would be the required level to qualify for selection, while "Desired" would be what the USAAC would hope to see.

where Monocoupe Corporation had previously built small private aircraft, directly across the runway from the massively expanded new facilities of Curtiss-Wright.

When the contractors' submittals were reviewed and ranked, the documenting report described their evaluations in three categories.

- Class 1, "Designs which are essentially modifications of existing production designs."
- Class 2, "Designs which are a departure from conventional designs but are sufficiently proven to justify expectation of production in 1942."
- Class 3, "Designs which are either conventional or unconventional but which depend largely on an extended power plant development program prior to the airplanes [sic] construction."

The USAAC had expected to receive as many as 100 responses to R40-C's ambitious requirements from these contractors. It would like to have seen designs that covered the widest possible spectrum of fighter-type aircraft, from refinements of existing types to radical designs employing cutting-edge ideas and technologies. Unfortunately, only 26 submittals were made, most of which were variations on a few baseline configurations with different engine and armament options. From this field, the USAAC evaluation team selected just three winners. They would become the Vultee XP-54, Curtiss-Wright XP-55, and Northrop XP-56, a nice array of different approaches to airframe/engine integration: a huge twin-boom aircraft, a medium-size canard layout, and a flying wing with bulbous fuselage and counter-rotating propellers.

Interestingly, all three aircraft featured pusher propellers, which had always been in and out of vogue for various reasons since the dawn of flight. Why the USAAC would put all of their figurative eggs in the "pusher" basket after the seriously disappointing performance of the twin-pusher Bell YFM-1 Airacuda is hard to understand, but there was a belief that pusher propellers were slightly more efficient than tractors, and they left the fighter's forward fuselage completely unobstructed for mounting armament without the complications involved in interrupter mechanisms. A concentration of guns there was felt to be more desirable than a spread of the same number in the wings, outboard of a tractor propeller's arc. The latter had to be aimed to converge at some distance ahead of the aircraft, beyond which the projectile density on target would be more spread out, while nose-mounted guns delivered a concentrated wave of projectiles at all ranges.

McDonnell had submitted its Model 1, also a pusher layout, but unlike the other entries it had two propellers that were driven by a single large engine buried in the fuselage, via driveshafts and right-angle gearboxes. McDonnell actually made four bids, using the same basic airframe concept but with each option using a different engine. The records of the evaluation committee, however, show that just two of these submittals were actually considered. The other two were "disregarded as a result of a preliminary engineering analysis of the data submitted" because "[t]he performance on McDonnell Aircraft Corporation Bids 3 and 4 was below the minimum specified in Type Specification AC-622 even with engines of [illegible, either 1650 or 1850] and 2350 horsepower, respectively."

The first of the "allowed" concepts' engines, Allison's V-3420, was an R40-A contender that had been rejected by the committee for pursuit-type aircraft as being unable to be installed due to its excessive size. Mounted in the nose or a conventional nacelle, that might have been true, but McDonnell showed that mounting it in the widest part of the center fuselage was another thing entirely. It fit there, it had the horsepower of two normal engines, and so it was possible to sculpt a relatively small fighter around it. It featured a two-stage gear-driven supercharger to improve high-altitude performance.

The second engine in the note, Pratt & Whitney's H-3130, had been studied by the US Navy several years earlier but was not submitted for R40-A. It seems to have offered considerably more power and higher performance at altitude than the V-3420 thanks to its two-stage, two-speed, gear-driven supercharger, but that extra performance would have come with a significant weight increase.

Regardless of which engine might be selected, the aircraft's projected performance did not compare favorably with other competitors and it finished near the bottom of the rankings. However, the USAAC was intrigued with the aircraft's unusual features, not just the interesting (and eventually patented) propeller drivetrain, but also the overall shape of the aircraft. McDonnell had applied a technique known as "blending" to an extreme degree: instead of having wings that met the fuselage with a modest fillet to streamline the join, the Model 1's fillet began at the top of the fuselage and ran smoothly out and down from there.

Such things had been done before in order to gain interior volume while theoretically maintaining some sort of airfoil-approximating lifting surface from centerline out to wingtip. The idea had been patented in 1921 by Nicolas Woyevodsky and then explored by the British company Miles in several projects.

Of most relevance to McDonnell's Model 1, however, was an American design that preceded it by approximately two years, and that provenance is crucial in understanding the entire history of the XP-67 because it came from the company where James S. McDonnell and a group of designers and engineers were working at the time, the Glenn L. Martin Company in Baltimore. In the late 1930s they had created two twin-engine bombers, the Baltimore and Maryland, that would be used primarily by the French and British air forces in the upcoming war. In the aircraft business, the completion of one design for production is immediately followed by brainstorming for the next generation. McDonnell's team took the general layout of the Maryland/Baltimore family and applied the extreme blending shown by Woyevodsky and Miles to create two progressively radical derivatives. First was the Martin Model 176, whose lines were clearly those of the earlier Maryland with blending added. From this stepping-stone came the much-refined Model 178, another twin-engine bomber but with blending carried much farther.

The original blueprint for the Model 178 wind-tunnel test model has survived in the Ron Farver Collection. The name on the blueprint is Ron's father, Lyle Farver, who would go on to become one of the original dozen employees of the new McDonnell Aircraft Corporation when "Mr Mac" made the break from Martin in 1939.

At this point, things were looking up for the new McDonnell Aircraft Corporation. No better engines would be available than those generated under R40-A, and the USAAC was definitely interested in the kind of design layout represented by MAC's Model 1. It decided to pay McDonnell for the engineering data package for that aircraft – the standard $3,000 that had been set at the beginning of the R40-C effort for payment to any contractor in a situation like this. (The same amount had also been paid to Northrop, Vultee, and Curtiss-Wright St Louis for their winning R40-C submittals.) Recognizing the potential of the USAAC interest, and unwilling to give up on a possible production opportunity, McDonnell began to work with the it on a process of refinement to develop Model 1 into something that might win a contract and be turned into flying hardware.

McDonnell had the foresight to assemble a highly qualified team to do the detailed design of the aircraft. A few names recur constantly in the program correspondence between MAC and the USAAC: McDonnell himself, of course, since he took an active role in launching his first-ever fighter; and Lyle Farver, who has already been mentioned

Martin Model 178, the direct ancestor of the McDonnell Model 1 and 2. (Ron Farver Collection)

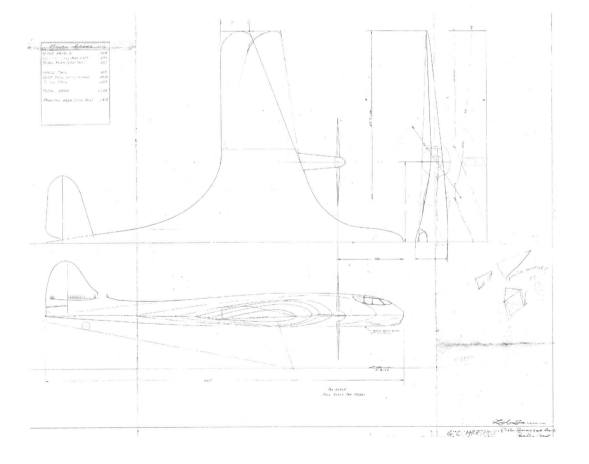

in connection with the genesis of the design concept, first at Glenn L. Martin and then at MAC. There is also Garrett C. Covington Jr, who was at first Assistant Chief Engineer in the Engineering Division, but in 1943 became its head, as the XP-67 was being built. Abraham Wyatt's name appears on many drawings thanks to his position as Chief of Structural Engineering, as does that of Kendall Perkins, one of the project engineers.

As Model 1 was being refined, MAC was expanding its facilities and personnel. It was successful in getting contracts to make components and subassemblies for other companies, which kept the lights on and the payroll funded. The largest of these contracts were engine cowls for Douglas's A-20 attack bomber and entire empennages for C-47s. The company also opened a plant in Memphis, Tennessee, where the AT-21 twin-engine gunnery trainer was built. That operation had to be shut down as quickly as it was set up when the USAAC abruptly cancelled; such were the risks run by manufacturers in the hectic days of World War II.

But despite the Memphis setback, MAC was doing amazingly well for itself, considering how briefly it had been in existence. Reading between the lines of contemporary correspondence, the company's success was certainly aided by the fact that better-known (at the time) aircraft companies were running at maximum capacity in a race to meet the dramatically increased production targets that the Roosevelt Administration had put in place as America entered World War II. If the USAAC wanted a new high-speed interceptor, the usual sources were tied up on other projects, with neither the engineering resources nor production space to explore other areas. But thanks to its founder's shrewd foresight, MAC offered a skilled, trained workforce and expanding factory space, centrally located in the country, having easy road, rail, air, and even barge transportation facilities at hand. Supplies and parts could be readily brought in, and products just as easily shipped out, in a variety of ways. With the capacity to take on work, and a close working relationship with the USAAC on its early Model 1 concept, MAC stood poised to make its mark.

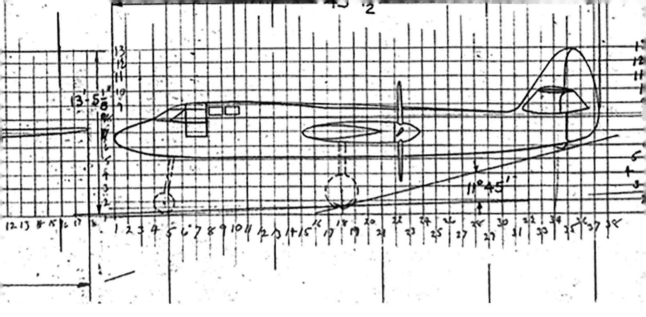

CHAPTER TWO

PROTOTYPE DESIGN

Request for Data R40-C was answered by McDonnell with "Model 1," developed through a myriad of sketches like this that shared a common overall configuration but that varied in many dimensions and details. Model 2 would follow, refined into Model 2A and finally XP-67, by which point R40-C's starting point had been left far behind. (Ron Farver Collection)

The design of Model 1's airframe and its propulsion system were extensively recorded in the form of Design Patents, as was common among aircraft companies at the time. This could and did lead to security problems. The Northrop XP-56, also initiated under R40-C, was similarly covered by design patents that anyone could retrieve and view despite the program's military security classification. This caused annoyance in the program's USAAC oversight offices due to a series of articles written about its features in the popular press at the time, based on the patent information. But McDonnell, possibly because it was a virtually unknown company at the time, seems to have avoided such problems with Model 1 and its successors despite the existence of patents.

An odd thing about these patents is that only one name is shown as "Inventor" – the founder of the new company, James S. McDonnell. However, information has come to light that casts serious doubt on that sole attribution. As noted earlier, drawings of the Martin 178 point toward Lyle Farver as being that aircraft's designer. Since the two aircraft are so similar it is reasonable to assume that he had an equally important role in developing Model 1. Another member of the original MAC crew, Charles Marschner, recalled in 2003 that "[i]n late 1939, Lyle Farver proposed the blended wing configuration to McDonnell Aircraft for presentation to the U.S. Army Air Corps . . . As I recall, Lyle Farver picked up the concept from a British design (possibly Miles) of 1938 or earlier." That strongly suggests that Farver was, in fact, the originator of Model 1's shape, and thus of its descendants down to XP-67 (and beyond), regardless of whose name was on the Design Patent application.

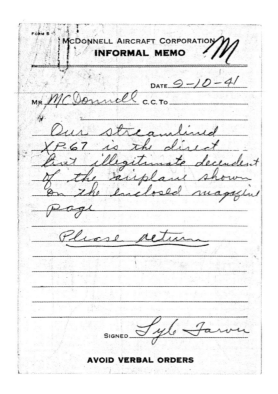

A telling confirmation of this has survived in the form of what McDonnell employees were decades later still calling "AVOs," because of the admonition carried on each one to "Avoid Verbal Orders." Sent by Lyle Farver to Mr Mac, after Model 1 had evolved into XP-67, its purpose seems to have been to let the latter know exactly where the aircraft had sprung from. It would be odd for a subordinate to send such a note to the creator himself. It seems more likely that Mr Mac,

Note from Lyle Farver to James S. McDonnell, to explain the genesis of the ultra-blended configuration that became XP-67. (Ron Farver Collection)

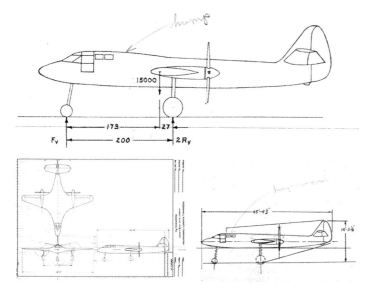

Original design sketches show variations that were explored for Model 1: different dihedral angles for horizontal tails with arrows added by authors, different contours for vertical tail with arrows again added, "hump" or "hump removed" over cockpit area. (Ron Farver Collection)

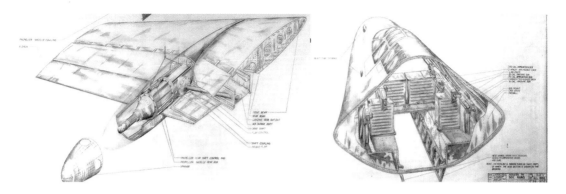

As these drawings show, Model 1 was far more than just a notional concept. It had been completely designed down to details of structure, armament, and even armor by the time it was proposed to the USAAC under R40-C. To have completed the design of a totally new aircraft within nine months of forming a new company with a small initial staff of designers and analysts was a truly remarkable achievement for McDonnell, that makes it easy to understand the USAAC's willingness to pay $3,000 for Model 1's design data even though the aircraft itself was not selected as a winner in the competition. (US Government source)

who after all had a business to set up, staff, and run, would not have been in the design loop personally, but would be getting information on the status of those designs from the people who were actually creating them. It seems plausible, given all of this, that Model 1 owed its existence primarily to Lyle Farver.

Model 1's evolution can be traced via subtle changes that abound in other sketches in the Ron Farver Collection. Addition or deletion of a "hump" over the cockpit, barely visible erasure lines where contours have been changed, and changing ground angle lines for landing gear geometries can be seen. Space limitations prevent showing them all, but a sample is given here.

Ultimately, Model 1's original design developed into something known today by its original MAC drawing number, "S-100." The most obvious differences from the original Model 1 are the wing planform, which has replaced the original swept leading edge/straight trailing edge with a more conventional layout, the "hump" over the cockpit area with a much cleaner looking canopy, and a ventral extension of the rear fuselage and rudder, presumably to both enhance directional stability and provide a skid for over-rotation on takeoffs or landings. These features would become part of all subsequent layouts.

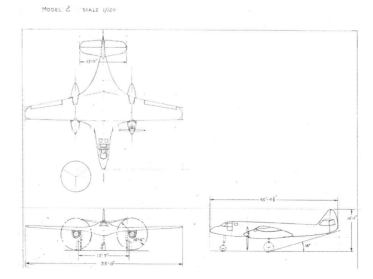

Model 2 layout. (Ron Farver Collection)

After the USAAC rejected Model 1, coordination with it led to a number of changes being made, and the follow-on Model 2 was a very different aircraft. While Model 1 had used a single engine with two-stage supercharger, buried in the fuselage to drive twin pusher propellers on the wing trailing edges, Model 2 adopted the thoroughly traditional approach of having separate engines in nacelles on the leading edges of the wings, driving tractor propellers. The engine selected for Model 2 was the Continental I-1430-1, described in Continental's contemporary documents as still having a two-stage supercharger at that point.

Pencil and pen sketches have survived to document the evolution of Model 2's basic layout. Model 1's final wing planform was retained, giving the entire aircraft a more mainstream appearance and marking a distinct step away from the earlier Martin Model 178. The wingspan, however, was significantly increased to carry conventional engine nacelles rather than the abbreviated housings for driveshafts that Model 1 used, with its single engine buried in the fuselage. While Model 1's wing/fuselage blending was retained, it was not initially extended to Model 2's new engine nacelles, which were simply faired into the wing in accordance with normal design practice. The un-fighter-like forward fuselage, however, was carried over mostly intact from Model 1. Probably reflecting the ex-Martin designers' familiarity with bomber cockpits, it would have had severe rearward visibility problems for any kind of fighter role.

As the drawing shows, the engine nacelles were initially hung under the wings, again following standard practices for bombers such as the B-24, B-25, and B-26, but oddly not the Baltimore or Maryland that the initial group of designers would have been most familiar with from their days at Glenn L. Martin. Wind tunnel testing on a 1/8th-scale model at the University of Detroit, however, showed problems. MAC Report Number 42 (April 16, 1941) gives a rare insight into how challenges are uncovered and dealt with in the aircraft design process: "Model 2 as originally designed had nacelles located below the wing with the engine very close to the center of gravity of the airplane, this

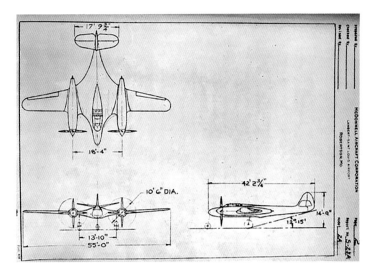

With Model 2A, the extreme wing/ fuselage blending became more fully developed. Extending from the top of the fuselage out over the nacelles and onto the outer wing panels, the ultimate in that direction would shortly be reached as 2A matured into the XP-67. (Ron Farver Collection)

Model 2A inboard profile drawing, marked "Preliminary" although no other seems to have survived. (Adapted by the authors from an original at the National Archives)

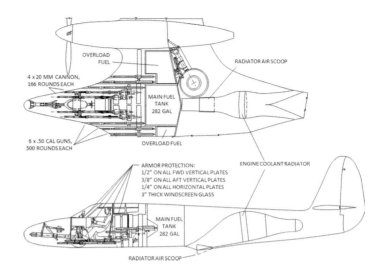

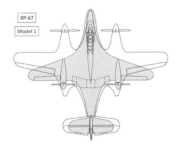

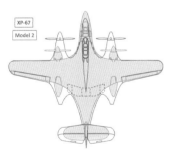

The path to the XP-67. (Authors' drawing)

arrangement being required for balance. The nacelle itself was designed to have the minimum wetted area, though in so doing the nacelle contours suffered as regards form drag. However, when the model was placed in the wind tunnel the drag increment due to the nacelles was found to be .0056 at low angles of attack and was accompanied by serious flow conditions at high angles of attack resulting in what was in effect an early stall. Consequently the nacelle design was changed and the nacelles themselves were made symmetrical about the wing chord line. An appreciable reduction of high speed drag was realized with this arrangement but the high angle of attack flow conditions remained serious. After considerable experimentation a satisfactory solution was reached by the use of blisters in the vicinity of the nacelles which resulted in a nacelle drag increment of .0045 and excellent flow conditions at high angles of attack."

These "blisters" were the beginnings of a process of extended blending, and it is significant that their addition gave a reduction in drag even though they increased wetted area, since a common criticism of the XP-67 is that its greater wetted area compared to conventionally shaped aircraft must have created higher drag.

This early series of tests even included consideration of how the aircraft's intended role might play into aerodynamic factors. MAC Report 42 noted: "Since the subject airplane is designed for high speeds at high altitude, careful pressure surveys were made over the whole model to determine whether the flow would exceed the velocity of sound at any point. These surveys indicate that no increase in drag due to the compressibility shock will be experienced on the full scale airplane, including the region of the nacelle where trouble would most logically be anticipated."

Model 2 was submitted to the USAAC on June 30, 1940, but like Model 1, failed to win a contract. Undeterred, McDonnell persisted. The basic design was refined, again with USAAC coordination, into Model 2A. (The wind-tunnel findings described above for Model 2 were specifically mentioned in MAC Report 42 as having been carried

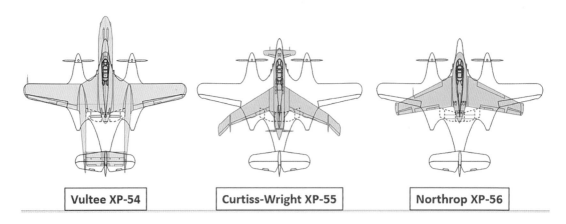

| Vultee XP-54 | Curtiss-Wright XP-55 | Northrop XP-56 |

forward into Model 2A.) Although its proportions were generally similar to those of Model 2, its fuselage forward of the wings was quite a bit shorter, and the bomber-type cockpit section was extensively redrawn to more closely resemble framed-canopy fighters of the period such as the P-38 and P-39. The blending of the wing, fuselage, and engine nacelles became more pronounced, building on Model 2's wind-tunnel results.

An excellent Inboard Profile drawing of Model 2A has survived, and a close look reveals some fascinating details. Most noticeably in section, but easily overlooked in three-views, is a large ventral scoop by which air was routed through giant internal ducts to provide cooling for the engine. The radiator was located in the rear fuselage, and air exited the aircraft via large exhaust openings behind it on each side.

Comparing the XP-67 with the other R40-C selectees shows just how widely they differed in size and configuration. While the XP-54 is similar in size, the other two appear almost toylike next to the XP-67. (Authors' drawing)

The only other aircraft that ever flew with the I-1430 engine, Lockheed's XP-49, was smaller and lighter than the XP-67 but had much larger propellers. (Authors' drawing)

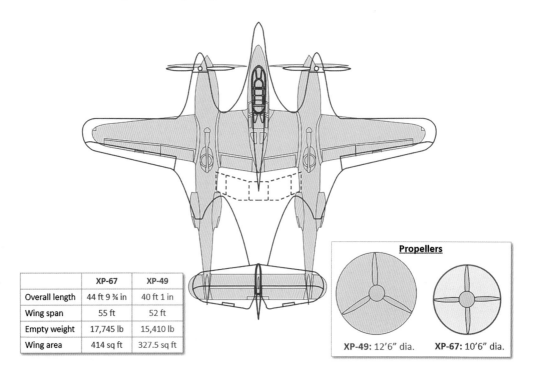

	XP-67	XP-49
Overall length	44 ft 9 ¾ in	40 ft 1 in
Wing span	55 ft	52 ft
Empty weight	17,745 lb	15,410 lb
Wing area	414 sq ft	327.5 sq ft

Propellers

XP-49: 12'6" dia.   XP-67: 10'6" dia.

A mockup under construction, March 19, 1942. No fancy jigs or holding fixtures, or even work stands, are in evidence, but the quality of the woodworking appears to be outstanding. Lyle Farver, originator of the extreme blended-surface concept at Glenn L. Martin and then MAC, is standing on the right. (Ron Farver Collection)

An impressive and warlike view for a fighter aircraft, showing the projected armament of three 37mm cannon on each side of the wing/fuselage interface. (Gerald Balzer Collection, Greater St Louis Air and Space Museum)

With the nose landing gear directly in front of it, it is easy to envision problems when operating on anything other than clean, dry, paved runways. Anything thrown up by that front wheel would almost inevitably end up being sucked into the inlet, with grave consequences.

Also of interest is the armament, consisting of six .50cal machine guns and four 20mm cannon, a potent amount of firepower for the day. All normal fuel was carried in a single centerline tank, with a smaller tank on each side for "overload" fuel. Harking all the way back to Model 1, the pilot was virtually surrounded by armor plate.

Model 2A was submitted to the USAAC on April 24, 1941, and MAC finally had a winner. Contract W535-AC-21218 called for two aircraft, a mock-up, various wind-tunnel models, a full-scale engine nacelle for testing, final data, and reports, all on a cost-plus-fixed-fee basis. The first aircraft was thought to be capable of delivery 18 months after contract signing and the second six months after that. Authority for Purchase 182428 was then issued, and the official designation XP-67 was assigned to the program.

There was a slight glitch up front when McDonnell's aircraft was inadvertently assigned the wrong X-number. Lt Col F. O. Carroll, Chief of the Experimental Engineering Section at the time, sent an airmail letter to McDonnell Aircraft on July 26, 1941, containing the following: "During the discussion of the Model Specification covering the detail requirements of the subject airplane, your representative, Mr. Covington, was told to refer in the specification to this airplane as the Air Corps Model XP-66. It has since been determined that this model designation was in error and Model XP-67 should be used." XP-66, of course, had been assigned to Vultee.

As with many new programs, there were challenges to be overcome. The question of exactly why the USAAC thought that there might be a need for something in this class was raised very early. Fortunately, it had answers ready, as can be seen from surviving correspondence from the period. A Routing and Record Sheet dated September 12, 1941, from the Chief of Air Corps to the Chief of Army Air Forces offered this: "In addition to obtaining an airplane possessing the above desirable characteristics, an opportunity is presented for developing another source of supply for airplanes of this type." This is a reference to the fact that other fighter makers were fully occupied in fulfilling orders and had no excess production capacity to devote to new products. Another Routing and Record Sheet, from the Pursuit Board to the Chief of Materiel Division, recommended that the project go ahead for various reasons, including "[t]he fact that no other airplane of comparable performance characteristics is now under development, particularly in respect to range. The Board believes that there is a definite need for an airplane of these characteristics in the pursuit development program." Also mentioned was "[t]he strategic mobility of this type due to its 2100 mile maximum range." This approaches the range needed to fly from the West Coast of the United States to Hawaii, so the mobility/deployability argument might have been persuasive as opposed to the only alternative, deploying the aircraft by ship. Yet another reason was, "The possible need for a fighter which can be employed on air alert or on distant patrol beyond the effective range of the conventional interceptor." The longer a fighter can loiter on patrol station, the fewer aircraft have to be in the inventory, giving a cost savings for the force as a whole.

With such high-level support, the XP-67 was given the green light, and MAC was in the fighter business that it would soon come to dominate.

Model 2A quickly lost its belly scoop and the associated ducting, which were replaced by large and elegantly sculpted intake ducts in the wing leading edges and large exhaust ducts at the rear end of each nacelle. The ultimate in blending was finally achieved, as it was extended from the top of the fuselage out and down to the inboard wing sections, then up and over the engine nacelles and finally back down and out to the outboard wing panels.

Less obvious changes included shortening the nose (although a subsequent mock-up review finding suggested lengthening it by 15in. to improve the mounting possibilities for the gunsight). The armament was changed to a battery of six 37mm cannon, all mounted in the fuselage. The horizontal tail was enlarged, as were the ailerons. Although many things changed, the aircraft is recognizably a refinement of Model 2A.

The development path between the original Model 1 and the XP-67 can best be traced by comparing the final product with each of its predecessors:

Section cuts through a nacelle show not just blending with the wing, but the complex ductwork and major components associated with the engines. (Traced from drawing in Ron Farver Collection)

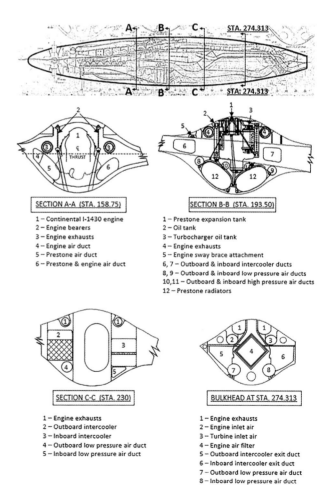

SECTION A-A (STA. 158.75)

1 – Continental I-1430 engine
2 – Engine bearers
3 – Engine exhausts
4 – Engine air duct
5 – Prestone air duct
6 – Prestone & engine air duct

SECTION B-B (STA. 193.50)

1 – Prestone expansion tank
2 – Oil tank
3 – Turbocharger oil tank
4 – Engine exhausts
5 – Engine sway brace attachment
6, 7 – Outboard & inboard intercooler ducts
8, 9 – Outboard & inboard low pressure air ducts
10,11 – Outboard & inboard high pressure air ducts
12 – Prestone radiators

SECTION C-C (STA. 230)

1 – Engine exhausts
2 – Outboard intercooler
3 – Inboard intercooler
4 – Outboard low pressure air duct
5 – Inboard low pressure air duct

BULKHEAD AT STA. 274.313

1 – Engine exhausts
2 – Engine inlet air
3 – Turbine inlet air
4 – Engine air filter
5 – Outboard intercooler exit duct
6 – Inboard intercooler exit duct
7 – Outboard low pressure air duct
8 – Inboard low pressure air duct

DIMENSIONS	MODEL 1	MODEL 2	MODEL 2A (MAC DRAWING S-10037, MAY 1941)	XP-67 (MAC DRAWING SK-346, APRIL 1943)
Length	45ft 4½in.	42ft 2in.	42ft 2¾in.	44ft 9¾in.
Wingspan	45ft	55ft	55ft	55 ft 13/8in.
Height, from ground	14ft 21/8in.	14ft ½in.	14ft 9in.	14ft 9in.
Height, from bottom of fuselage (datum line)	(No data)	(No data)	10ft 7¼in.	9ft 1in.
Wing area (including ailerons)	(No data)	(No data)	414 sq ft	414 sq ft
Wing aspect ratio	(No data)	(No data)	7.3	7.3
Wing dihedral	(No data)	(No data)	(No data)	5°
Wing taper ratio	(No data)	(No data)	(No data)	2.37:1
Wing mean aerodynamic chord (MAC)	(No data)	(No data)	(No data)	8ft 4in.
Wing airfoil	(No data)	(No data)	(No data)	NACA 66,2-213.631
Horizontal tail span	16ft 5½in.	17ft 9¾in.	17ft 9¾in.	20ft 4in.
Horizontal tail dihedral	(No data)	(No data)	(No data)	8°36'34"
Horizontal tail surface area	(No data)	(No data)	(No data)	103.6 sq ft
Vertical [tail] surface area	(No data)	(No data)	(No data)	58.23 sq ft
Nacelle separation	(No data)	18ft 4in.	18ft 4in.	18ft 4in.
Maximum ground angle	17°	12°15'	12°15'	12°30'
Wheel base	16ft 8in.	(No data)	(No data)	15ft 8½in.
Wheel track	17ft 10in. to 19ft 1¾in.	13ft 10in.	13ft 10in.	17ft 9½in.
Propeller diameter	10ft 6in.	10ft 6in.	10ft 6in.	10ft 6in.[1]
Propeller gear ratio	(No data)	(No data)	1:2.771	1:2.277
Flap deflection angle	(No data)	(No data)	45°	45°[2]

(1) XP-67 Final Report shows 10ft 8in. but all other sources show 10ft 6in., so this is believed to be a typo
(2) Taken from Jan–Mar 1942 drawing 2-00000 "General Arrangement Interceptor-Pursuit"

It is also interesting to look at how the XP-67 compares with the other aircraft that came out of the original R40-C submittals: XP-54, XP-55, and XP-56. Despite the fact that Model 1 was generated against that request, its subsequent development and refinement into the XP-67 clearly put quite a bit of distance between it and the three declared winners of the original competition. No longer a single-engine pusher fighter, it had matured into a twin-engine heavy fighter-interceptor.

A final comparison is worth making as well. Only one other aircraft besides XP-67 ever flew with the Continental I-1430 engine, and that was Lockheed's enlarged P-38 follow-on, the XP-49. Strangely though, the XP-67, despite being larger and heavier, had significantly smaller-diameter propellers. Despite having four blades rather than three, the total disk area was a full 30 percent smaller. This should be kept in mind when later flight test shortcomings are described.

A wooden mockup was used to develop the main features of the design before committing parts to production, and to verify with the customer that factors such as equipment location, pilot visibility, accessibility of components, and overall layout were acceptable.

A few changes had been made while the mockup was being constructed, the most noticeable of which was that the original scheme

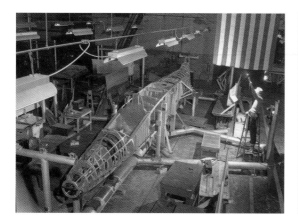

for retracting the main landing gear had been changed for a curious reason. At the time, there was a *Handbook of Instructions for Airplane Designers* and apparently its provisions were considered to be firm requirements, because when its Revision 5 promulgated new "angle and take-off requirements" (according to the XP-67 Final Report) "it was necessary to completely redesign the landing gear and nacelles so that the gear would retract into the engine nacelles instead of the wing." This must have led to delays for redesign and re-engineering; it is hard to understand why the existing design would not have been considered to be "grandfathered in" at the time, rather than pushing back what was being touted as an urgently needed type of aircraft for the USAAC, or at least holding the changes in abeyance for the second prototype, as so many other things subsequently would be. Another modification, based on wind-tunnel testing, included changing the ailerons from Frise balance to internal balanced and sealed. The process seems to have been an illustration of the saying that "better is the enemy of good enough," but in the end, the mockup was completed to reflect the desired configuration features.

Above left
Construction of the fuselage at an early stage. The strictly conventional longeron/rib type structure is reminiscent of "stick-built" model aircraft of the day. The cockpit "tub" appears to be an integrated module, in keeping with the pressurization that it was supposed to offer, but which was never fitted to the XP-67. The photographer's assistant is just under the flag, providing supplemental illumination. (Gerald Balzer Collection, Greater St Louis Air and Space Museum)

Above right
A red-letter day: joining the inner wing panel to the fuselage. The upper fuselage skin that was being held on with cleco fasteners has been removed here, presumably to preserve access to underlying areas as long as possible while subsystem components are fitted. (Gerald Balzer Collection, Greater St Louis Air and Space Museum)

Fuselage construction is proceeding nicely. Massive engine mounts ("bearers") are on both sides. Openings for 37mm guns are also evident, although armament was never actually fitted to the XP-67. These holes would be covered up and painted over, not to become visible again until the disastrous fire that ended the program. (Gerald Balzer Collection, Greater St Louis Air and Space Museum)

The I-1430 engine in XP-67's left nacelle shows a maze of ducting and associated items, with much more hidden behind and under what can be seen here. Identification and arrows added by authors. (Ron Farver Collection)

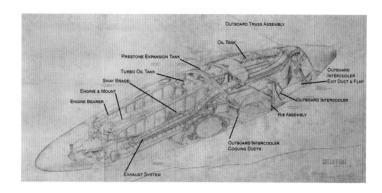

An inspection of the mockup was held on April 15–17, 1942 and, despite the coordination in advance, was said by the Final Report to have "resulted in a large number of detailed changes" which notably included "a request for provisions for the type BM turbo supercharger as an alternate for the type D-2 and a request for a 15 inch extension of the fuselage nose to improve gun sight vision." The MAC-designed pushrod flight control system was also recommended to be changed to a cable version.

That was a general preference among the services at the time, for a reason that was directly related to combat survivability, and not just in America. About two years before XP-67's mockup review, No. 71 Sqn of the Royal Air Force had been asked to comment on the Brewster Buffalo fighters it had been issued with. Sqn Ldr Walter Churchill, had this to say about pushrod-activated flight controls, "While this is a positive method of operation it is feared that an explosive shell or even a bullet . . . may shatter or collapse it. Experience has proved how much punishment the twin cable can stand without breaking down." When this report was forwarded to the US Navy's Bureau of Aeronautics, it contained this further comment from an Ens George Gibson (USNR), "There are bullets in this war, and the more area occupied by any part, the greater is the possibility that it will be hit." One of the authors of this book spent several decades working in the field of combat aircraft opportunity, and would like to point out that both pushrods and cables are very lightly loaded, so both approaches can be equally survivable against most threats. It should also be noted that the P-47 Thunderbolt, universally regarded as a very "tough" and survivable aircraft, employed pushrods and bellcranks in its flight controls rather than cables. Nevertheless, this is further proof, along with the previously mentioned provision for extensive armor as far back as Model 1, and the gunfire testing programs that would ultimately be done on certain XP-67 components, that this was not just a program to determine the performance potential of a highly

Inboard and outboard sides of an I-1430 engine upon arrival at McDonnell. In the lower photograph, a blueprint of the supercharger is spread open on the work surface. (Ron Farver Collection)

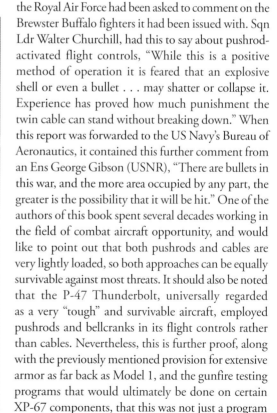

Beginning the process of installing an I-1430 engine. (Gerald Balzer Collection, Greater St Louis Air and Space Museum)

blended laminar-flow airframe; it was aimed from the outset at producing a viable combat-ready design.

The mockup review board's report was sent to MAC, and the Model Specification was updated to reflect the desired changes. It was also decided that the engines to be used would be the I-1430-17 and -19, rather than -1. These were "handed" engines, meaning that one rotated clockwise and the other counterclockwise. One of the more interesting outcomes of subsequent wind-tunnel stability testing would directly bear on this fact, but at this point those tests were in the future. The engine replacement simply made it possible to have propellers that both rotated either up or down toward the fuselage, besides offering other technical upgrades made by Continental since the I-1430-1 stage. The -17 and -19 engines featured single-stage, single-speed mechanically driven superchargers as well as single-stage exhaust-driven turbosuperchargers.

A ground-firing mockup section representing the three 37mm guns and surrounding structure on the right side had also been built by MAC, and firing tests were done on it at Wright Field from May 26–June 4, 1942. Enough damage ensued to prove that the structure needed more blast protection, which is not an uncommon outcome in a new aircraft's early engineering.

Drawings were rolling out of MAC for every part of the aircraft by this point, and being provided to the USAAC for review and comment. In general, these comments seem to have been positive, although not infrequently modifications were required based on standard design practices and expected service environments. Analyses of the XP-67's control characteristics and performance estimates were also being made, in conjunction with the ongoing wind-tunnel testing. It must have been a tricky proposition, balancing all of these potential sources of changes with the realities of schedule and cost, but all successful programs must solve the same puzzles early in their lives.

The caption on the back of this photo reads "carburetor elbow and oil 'Y' drain," although there are obviously many other things running through this shared space. (Ron Farver Collection)

Right
Engine oil breather lines, looking forward along the top of the engine. Note that someone has put a big label on a propeller blade (top right of photo) saying "Don't move prop." (Ron Farver Collection)

Far right
Prestone (engine coolant) surge tank and miscellaneous upper plumbing, looking aft. The engine supercharger housing is the ribbed circle below the tank. (Ron Farver Collection)

What appear in photos to be simple twin nozzles actually consists of a maze of components associated mostly with keeping the nacelles cool. The original caption on this photo reads "Turbo installation – outboard." The labeling is on the original photo. (Ron Farver Collection)

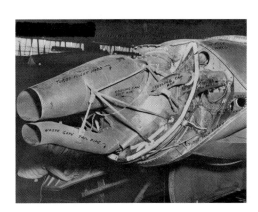

At the heart of the design were the I-1430 engines, and how they were integrated with the aircraft and its control systems. All of the various propulsion system operations required a highly complex network of intake, flow-through, and exhaust components. The nacelles were carefully sculpted to be as small as possible while still being able to accommodate everything without resorting to drag-producing bumps and bulges.

Construction of the XP-67 was well documented in photographs, which show a normal progression from skeletal structures to completed subassemblies, which become major assemblies into which subsystem components were mounted before final assembly. The process has not changed much today, but what is noticeable about the XP-67's construction (in common with most aircraft of that period) is what would be considered extremely basic facilities and tools, as well as a complete absence of even the most rudimentary personal protective equipment. Yet during this time period, MAC's safety record was roughly twice as good as that of the industry as a whole, according to contemporary statistics.

Aluminum was used for most of the structure and outer skin, with stainless steel in places like the rear portions of the engine nacelles where service temperatures were expected to require it.

Engines were a pacing item in the construction process. Photos exist showing the arrival of the first engine at MAC, either one of the original engines fitted to the first prototype or possibly the engine that was installed in a full-size engine nacelle that was tested in wind tunnels at the National Advisory Committee for Aeronautics (NACA) wind tunnel at Langley, Virginia, and then at the tunnel at Wright Field. The results of those tests played a crucial role in solving serious cooling and drag problems associated with the initial design of the inlet and exhaust ducts.

Once installed into the airframe, it is again obvious how compactly arranged everything was, and yet even at this early stage, attention had been paid to maintainability of service versions. At the engine's 689[3]

---

3   A 689 inspection is scheduled when a new design or major change to an existing one is at the prototype stage, so that any deficiencies can be corrected before testing begins, and also so that changes can be recommended that would make future production and service use more efficient and effective, or improve safety to operators and maintainers.

inspection in late 1943, this subject was addressed, but possibly with less sense of urgency than would be normal, because by then, as the report's cover memo said, "This inspection was made with the understanding that in the event the XP-67 airplane is put into production, the nacelles will be redesigned around an engine other than the I-1430." The inspector's specific concerns in that regard centered around the supercharger, because "[t]his redesign may, if the engine selected is a two-stage engine, eliminate the turbo-supercharger." The knowledge that the engine itself would never see service must have somewhat cooled the reviewers' fervor for identifying maintainability issues overall.

The highly unusual inlet ducts were one of the XP-67's most dramatic and noticeable features from the front. Although appearing smooth and continuous, they were divided into flow paths for different functions Luckily, the NACA documented what each of these segments was for.

The XP-67's surviving photographs, as far as can be determined, exclusively pertain to the first prototype. The contract covered construction of two, but that changed, at least informally, due to the engine situation. By the time that construction started, it had become apparent that the I-1430 was never going to reach production, and some other propulsion solution would have to be found if the XP-67 was to succeed in being approved for adoption by the United States Army Air Force (USAAF). Unfortunately, the very nature of the aircraft worked against it; another engine could not just be dropped into the nacelles. On the XP-67, those nacelles

At about midpoint in construction, the engines are installed, but outer wing panels are yet to be added. Fuselage, inboard wings, and nacelles are not fully skinned. Landing gear is installed but the aircraft is still being supported by jack stands, so that gear retraction and extension can be tested. At the middle far right, upper and lower skins for one of the nacelles are shown, and a bit of upper wing skin, can just be seen sitting on the framed jig that represents the contours of the moldline in those areas. To the left of that, beyond the left main landing gear, is the corresponding jig for the other wing and nacelle, again with skins partially covering it. Looking at the aircraft itself, there is minimal use of expensive forgings; apart from the engine bearers, most load-bearing structures are built up from sheet and plate, mechanically fastened together to form stiffened structural elements. On the far left is the hydraulic power supply stand, used for ground testing systems; the hydraulic tubing is on the far side. (Gerald Balzer Collection, Greater St Louis Air and Space Museum)

Far left
The nose gear well is clean and uncluttered, before hydraulics are installed. (Gerald Balzer Collection, Greater St Louis Air and Space Museum)

Left
The left main gear well with fully installed hydraulics is ready for functional checkout. In the background on the right is the equipment for supplying pressurized hydraulic fluid to the aircraft without requiring engines to be started. The door-closing mechanism can be seen at the top center of the photo; it would turn out to cause nuisance problems in flight, as the doors tended to be pulled slightly open by slipstream air, thanks to the Bernoulli effect: higher air velocity equals lower static pressure, creating a suction on the doors. Note also, just to the left of the tire, the MAC negative number and date, October 24, 1943. (Gerald Balzer Collection, Greater St Louis Air and Space Museum)

November 29, 1943: the finished XP-67 shows its cleanly blended contours to best advantage in this front view. Taken from a slightly elevated position, it shows the inboard inlet ducts to good advantage. Most similar photos suffer obscuration of both the inboard and outboard ducts because virtually all of the ground shots have both propellers exactly like this, with blades straight up-and-down, left-and-right. While that makes for a crisp composition, it inevitably means that the blades cover up most or all of the inlets, which is frustrating for the modern-day researcher. Adjacent to the cockpit on the right side, a small flat-topped wedge has been temporarily attached to ease entry into and exit from the cockpit. The shape of the blended skin in that area made ingress and egress difficult, as test pilots would note in their reports on the aircraft about six months later. (Gerald Balzer Collection, Greater St Louis Air and Space Museum)

Inboard and outboard inlets were subdivided to feed air to specific things, as documented in an excellent set of images from NASA. (US Government source)

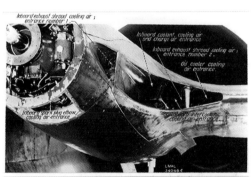

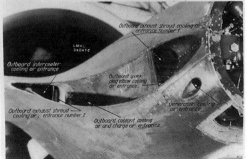

were carefully designed to be the minimum possible size that could fit around the I-1430 with all of the associated ducting and its turbosupercharger. Even so, pilot visibility would prove to be uncomfortably blocked to the sides, as USAAF flight testing would later bear out. The only other available American liquid-cooled engine option in 1943 would have been Allison's V-1710, and since the I-1430 had 27 percent less presented area from the front, the V-1710 would have required a substantially larger nacelle. That would have forced a redesign of not just the nacelle structure, but thanks to the XP-67's unique (for the time) use of extreme blending between nacelles and adjacent wing surfaces, those areas would have had to be re-engineered as well, and new jigs and tooling built to accommodate the extensive moldline and substructure changes that would have resulted. With larger nacelles, pilot visibility to the side would likely have gone from marginal to unacceptable, leading to a redesign of the cockpit area to raise the pilot's seat. Since that area was extensively blended front-to-back and side-to-side, redesign and retooling would have been necessary there, too. Weight and balance would have obviously been affected; more seriously, so would the crucial wind-tunnel findings by NACA and the USAAF regarding drag and cooling. More modifications would have had to be made to at least the ¼-scale model so that those tests could be rerun, and yet more delays incurred on top of those already encountered.

For all of these reasons, it was informally agreed to hold construction of Ship Two in abeyance pending the outcome of flight testing on Ship One. If the results were promising, and the USAAF showed interest in proceeding, then a production-relevant propulsion system would be incorporated as the next logical step in the development process. But since extensive structural changes were bound to be required, it made no sense to continue building the Ship One-type structure if it would only have to be disassembled and reconfigured later. Ship Two therefore remained untouched at about the 15 percent level of completion, while all eyes were fixed on Ship One as it prepared to begin its testing.

CHAPTER THREE

TEST AND DEVELOPMENT

XP-67 testing can be broken into three interdependent segments. First, beginning back in Model 1 days and already described to some extent for Model 2, there were wind-tunnel tests of various kinds. Initially intended to build up a database for answering basic questions to support fundamental configuration design, they became more concerned with specific problems involving lift, drag, stability, flying characteristics, and, critically for this aircraft, engine cooling. Second, there were hardware tests to validate tightly focused questions involving hardware, such as slosh testing of fuel tanks, gunfire testing of components, and flutter and vibration testing of the aircraft as a whole. Last, and of the greatest scope, was flight testing of the only completed prototype, to determine whether it met its guaranteed levels of performance.

Wind-tunnel testing involved a number of models that differed in size, configuration, and purpose. The XP-67 Final Report in 1946 contained a good overview of these models and their testing.

The main outcomes of all these tests were that the spin characteristics, which had been a source of concern due to the unique nature of the highly blended configuration, were found to be acceptable; longitudinal stability issues could be mostly alleviated by raising the XP-67's horizontal tail 12in.; and both engine cooling problems and higher than expected drag associated with the intakes on the wing leading edges could be greatly improved by resculpting those areas. Events during flight testing would prove those findings to be exceptionally well timed.

One report in particular deserves a closer look. Entitled "Longitudinal Stability of the McDonnell XP-67," regarding testing of the ¼-scale

The ¼-scale model embodied a number of features from Model 2A that were no longer relevant to the XP-67, such as the large movable exhaust cones visible here. This required extensive rework of the model, producing serious delays in the program and adding costs, the responsibility for which was settled by a Judge Advocate General decision in favor of McDonnell and against the USAAF. (Gerald Balzer Collection, Greater St Louis Air and Space Museum)

MODEL	WIND TUNNEL	PURPOSE	DATE TESTED
1/16 Scale, Complete Airplane (Model IIA)	Wright Field 5 Foot Tunnel	Determination of Aerodynamic Characteristics.	April, 1941
1/8 Scale, Complete Airplane (Model I revised to II A)	University of Detroit Tunnel	Determination of Aerodynamic Characteristics.	Intermittently during 1941
24" chord airfoil, 66, 2-213 and 24" chord airfoil, 66, 2-413	NACA Airflow Research Tunnel	Airfoil Pressure Distribution and Section Characteristics.	January, 1942
1/27 Scale, Spin Model (XP-67)	NACA 20 Foot Spin Tunnel	Determination of Spin Characteristics.	March, 1942
2/5 Scale, Wing & Aileron (XP-67)	NACA 7x10 Foot Tunnel	Aileron Development.	April, 1942
Full Scale, Practical Construction Wing (XP-67)	NACA Two Dimensional Tunnel	Determine nature of airflow over wing of practical construction.	August 1942 and April 1943
1/4 Scale, Complete Airplane Powered Model (XP-67)	NACA Propeller Research Tunnel	Determination of Aerodynamic Characteristics & design of duct entrances.	July – October, 1943
Full Scale, Powered Nacelle (XP-67)	NACA 16' Tunnel and Wright Field 20' Tunnel	Determination of engine operating characteristics and duct performance	July – August, 1943 and Oct., Nov., 1943

The summary of wind-tunnel test models shows a wide variety of testing, much of which proved invaluable to initial design and mid-program refinement. Critical changes were made to the XP-67 prototype as a result of these tests. (US Government source)

NACA testing showed substantial benefits for "Inlet revisions 3-C, 3-D and 3-E," which produced substantial drag reductions and phenomenal increases in cooling efficiency. (US Government source)

model, it was the subject of a Routing and Record Sheet from the Aerodynamics Branch, Aircraft Laboratory, Engineering Division to the Fighter Branch, Aircraft Projects Section that picked out some important points:

"Of the three variables tested, vertical position of the tail, plan-form of the wing, and duct-inlet shape, the change in tail position gave the most noticeable effect on longitudinal stability . . . After observation of all power-on results obtained to date it is concluded that this airplane cannot be made stable with the propellers revolving down in the center. Both full and half military power curves show complete instability with no sign of recovery. Having the stabilizer raised 3 inches gave the best all-around longitudinal stability to date, propellers rotating up through the center. Altering the duct-inlet shape had little or no effect on the stability. Removing the trailing edge inboard fillets increased the power-on stability at the expense of an increase in drag and a decrease in maximum lift. It is possible that improved fairing would eliminate the increase in drag." (When the report says 3in., it refers to an absolute measurement on the model. Since the model was ¼-scale, that translated to 12in. on the actual aircraft.)

The actual magnitude of improvement that testing of the ¼-scale model demonstrated is truly remarkable. Another letter, from October 1943, made the following observations: "The recent tests of the P-67 have given a fair promise of [normal] aerodynamic characteristics as to performance and stability and cooling providing the ducts and adjacent leading edges of the wing are modified considerably with respect to the original design. It is apparent that the changes made in the model ducts have reduced the drag by approximately 25 per cent at a lift coefficient of 7/10 while the potential cooling was increased over 200 per cent." In some ways, this extra cooling turned out to be a mixed blessing, but it was a sterling result, and much of this work would find its way directly into the configuration. However, first would come a short initial series of flight tests with the original aircraft geometry.

When the XP-67 prototype emerged into the crisp fall air for the first time in November 1943, it was quite an impressive sight. Nothing like it had ever been seen, certainly not in St Louis;

although just five months earlier, an equally weird-looking twin-boom prototype, also deriving from R40-C, had made its appearance just across the runway as Curtiss-Wright rolled out its XP-55 Ascender, and that first prototype had already been lost during flight testing.

A vibration and flutter survey was done from November 22–25, with "generally satisfactory" results. It is interesting to note that November 25 was Thanksgiving Day that year, which gives some idea of how motivated the program workers must have been.

The formal 689 inspection occurred from December 1–3. The Final Report says that the armament bay, lacking guns and ammunition stowage, had CO_2 bottles instead for "the special fire extinguisher system." The report also says there were many recommendations but none that required major modifications. That allowed taxi tests to begin on the heels of the inspection.

The taxi tests went well until fires broke out in both engine nacelles on December 8, and this is often cited as the beginning of chronic engine overheating and fire problems that would ultimately doom the aircraft. In fact, it was nothing of the sort. The fires were caused by failures of the exhaust manifold slip rings, which caused the manifolds to collapse, with the resulting hot air leaks setting the oil tanks on fire. It was the peripheral components servicing the engines that were to blame; the engines themselves were not involved. But the seed was planted, and the myth of engine unreliability soon became entrenched, even in USAAF circles.

The fires naturally caused a delay in the date of the first flight, but in any case, the USAAF did not actually approve MAC's flight test program plan until December 17. That approval contained a request that testing also include a determination of range, and that MAC coordinate the control and stability testing with Materiel Command. The last few weeks of 1943 were used to add a number of new vents to the upper sides of the nacelles, as well as pushing out the front portions of the

Two days before its 689 inspection, the XP-67 is on the MAC ramp for checkouts. In front of the aircraft, MAC's Chief Test Pilot, Ed Elliott (in overcoat, gloves, and hat), watches intently. (Gerald Balzer Collection, Greater St Louis Air and Space Museum)

Taxi test fires resulted in greatly enhanced flow-through ventilation provisions for engine and nacelle cooling before the XP-67's first flight on January 6, 1944, with a proliferation of new scoops and vents as well as enlargement of existing ones. Although they undoubtedly would add to the drag and therefore harm top speed numbers, it must have seemed preferable to do that than to risk losing the only flying prototype due to excessively high internal temperatures in the nacelles. (Gerald Balzer Collection, Greater St Louis Air and Space Museum)

November-December 1943
Front: Scoop on top and small scoop on right hand side of each nacelle.
Rear: No scoops or vents other than intercooler and engine exhausts.

Added or modified between taxi tests (12/3/1943) and first flight (1/6/1944)

1. Nacelle cooling air inlet
2. Generator cooling air inlet
3. Enlarged nacelle cooling air inlet
4. Enlarged inboard/outboard exhaust shroud cooling air inlet
5. Forward exhaust shroud exit air
6. Battery compartment exit air
7. Aft exhaust shroud exit air

The big day arrives at last. A group of civilians and military men await the flight. XP-67 Ship One is flanked left and right by fire extinguisher carts, a natural concern after dual engine nacelle fires during taxi testing. The small wedge-shaped block is still installed next to the cockpit. (Gerald Balzer Collection, Greater St Louis Air and Space Museum)

inboard and outboard inlet ducts (the exhaust shroud cooling intakes) so that they could capture air more effectively, and similarly enlarging the smaller forward-facing scoops at the very tops of the nacelles just behind the propeller spinners. The new vents were incidentally different in detail from ones that had been rather crudely made from sheet metal in the NACA and Dayton wind-tunnel experiments, but were clearly inspired by that work. The small intake for generator cooling air at the lower right side of each nacelle was apparently doing its job adequately, because it remained unchanged. MAC was obviously determined to learn from the taxi testing experience and hopefully head off any future overheating problems in the nacelles.

As had been the case with Curtiss-Wright's XP-55 a few months earlier, it was decided to begin flight testing at Scott Field, just across the Mississippi River from St Louis. Scott was relatively free from

the pressure of coordinating flights with commercial air traffic that would be inherent in operating from MAC's facility at Lambert Airport. The new XP-67 was trucked to Scott by road during late December, where it was made ready for its first flight.

Special high-visibility markings had been applied to the aircraft for easier visual and photographic tracking. MAC and USAAF spectators arrived on January 6, 1944 and there was a flurry of photo-taking prior to the first flight, including the first-ever photo of Mr Mac himself, standing proudly in front of his company's first all-new aircraft. It would be the progenitor of many more such photos in the 30-plus years to come.

Mr Mac with his new company's first fighter at Scott Field on January 6, 1944, giving a good view of the nose and tail stripe markings used on test flights. (Gerald Balzer Collection, Greater St Louis Air and Space Museum)

This flight, as well as virtually all others, was flown by a recent addition to the MAC organization, Everett Edward "Ed" Elliott, who had come from Curtis-Wright's Buffalo plant where he flew P-40 fighters and C-46 transports. He had previously been a US Navy pilot doing test work at Anacostia, in Washington, DC, where he flew every type of naval aircraft at the station. That was followed by a stint with a torpedo-bomber squadron aboard the aircraft carrier USS *Saratoga* CV-3, then a year with a fighter squadron aboard the USS *Lexington* CV-2, and assignment to a patrol bomber squadron. With this wide spectrum of experience behind him, Elliott's arrival was a lucky break for MAC.

MAC Chief Test Pilot E. E. "Ed" Elliott suited up and ready to go. He is holding a true protective helmet rather than the cloth or leather ones that were universal until Northrop test pilot John Myers' life was saved by his polo helmet in the crash of the first XP-56 a few months earlier. Apparently, his example was quickly adopted by others in the test piloting community. (Gerald Balzer Collection, Greater St Louis Air and Space Museum)

Unfortunately, the first flight had serious problems. Takeoff was followed by one circuit of the field and then an emergency landing, totaling just six minutes in the air. The problem again involved thermal failures of parts in both nacelles. Once again, they are popularly referred to as "engine fires," which gives a misleading impression. As with the taxi test incident, it was actually the peripheral equipment that caused the problems. The USAAFs Power Plant Laboratory did an investigation and their report notes: "Damage to the secondary aluminum structure of the tail cone was considerable and the supercharger regulators and waste gate linkage suffered damage . . . The cause of the overheating in the turbo compartments was apparently the result of low pressure in the open wheel wells which communicate to the turbo supercharger compartments. There was evidence of exhaust gas back-flow from the supercharger flight hoods through the tail cone sections and through the wheel well."

The report makes a number of recommendations, one of which was to become prominently visible on subsequent flights: "Cut off the rear section of the tail cone about eight inches ahead of the turbo supercharger flight hood." This would result in

E-2310 1-6-44

The left nacelle shroud shows melting and distortion after the first flight. (Gerald Balzer Collection, Greater St Louis Air and Space Museum)

both the turbo flight hood and waste gate tailpipe protruding well beyond the rear of the engine nacelles. Another change would be visible from certain angles, but much less so than the cutoffs: "Provide louvers for discharging the cooling air in the section of the tail cone ahead of the firewall. Two of these louvers should be located on the upper portion of the tail cone and one on the bottom portion of the tail cone directly beneath the compressor casing."

These recommendations would be acted on in due time, but immediately after the flight there was only the squawk sheet to reveal the extent of the damage, none of which was severe but all requiring attention before the next flight could be planned. Despite all of this, the program's official Case History says that "the airplane handled very well and that the landing speed and roll were shorter than anticipated."

While the results from this first flight were being evaluated, a highly significant series of conversations were being conducted between MAC and the USAAF that would affect the entire future of the XP-67 program and its potential for reaching production. Capt John Aldridge Jr was the focus on the customer side, while Garrett Covington and James McDonnell represented MAC. It had previously been acknowledged that the Continental I-1430 was not going into production, which was a genuine problem for an aircraft that had literally been designed around that engine, and whose unusual contours meant that a different engine could not just be dropped into the same space. The whole reason for the I-1430's existence was to pack as much power as possible into as small a space as could be managed; engines of comparable or greater power were too large to make a simple swap feasible. If I-1430s were not going to be available, then a major redesign was going to be needed to take the XP-67 out of the "X" category and make it a viable production aircraft. At the same time, jet engines were suddenly looking more realistic for future combat aircraft, despite significant drawbacks with their fuel consumption and limited thrust giving lackluster acceleration. A brief era was dawning when "mixed propulsion" concepts, using a piston engine for cruise efficiency but adding a jet for high speed dash and extra thrust during takeoff, were being considered by many aviation companies. One of them, the Ryan FR-1 Fireball, actually made it into limited production, so this was not a crazy idea at the time.

MAC had already been given a secret contract with the US Navy to create a pure jet fighter. In that connection, McDonnell made a visit to Britain to be briefed on the status of engines there. It seems only natural that he would have used that knowledge to help overcome the propulsion system dilemma with the XP-67, and in fact by mid-1943 there were preliminary drawings of a modified XP-67 featuring two options for piston engines (Allison or Rolls-Royce) in the front of each nacelle and a jet engine in the rear. McDonnell wasted no time in making the USAAF aware of the concept.

An Inter-Office Memorandum (IOM) on January 19, 1944, from Aldridge to the Chief of Aircraft Projects at Wright Field on "XP-67 Status," gives a good idea of how it was received, as well as the engine issue's effect on the just-started second XP-67 prototype: "[T]he Project Officer discussed with Mr. McDonnell and Mr. Covington a proposed program for the second airplane. It appears that this airplane has very good possibilities of meeting the tactical needs for very long range and heavy fire power. . . [It] appears wasteful to bring out the second airplane with the Continental engine, for if production were considered no prototype would be available. This is not intended as a reflection on the Continental engine, as it is the opinion of this office that the engine has performed satisfactorily. This opinion is borne out by tunnel tests of the full-scale nacelle at Wright Field, during which engine difficulties were practically non-existant [sic] and the engine delivered its rated 1600 hp for protracted periods of time. Nevertheless, in view of the feeling that come what may, there is no chance of further engines of this type being built, an engine change in the second airplane is the most advisable move to make. McDonnell proposes to make this change to either an Allison two-stage engine or the Rolls-Royce 14SM engine.

Along with installation of one of these alternate types of engines, McDonnell proposes to install J-32 Westernhouse [sic] Jet Unit in the space now occupied by the turbo in each engine nacelle. Performance figures with the 14SM engine and the jet unit are quite good . . . This proposal was presented to General Carroll who directed that the matter be held in abeyance pending clarification of the engine allocation picture. Mr. McDonnell wanted to have the program approved at once as he feels that he has man-power available to start work immediately,

The actual squawk sheet describing in detail the damage suffered to the aircraft during its abbreviated first flight. It is apparent that the problems were worse for the left nacelle than for the right one, a fact which is borne out by physical evidence. Item 4 is most likely the damage shown in the photograph on page 41. (Greater St Louis Air and Space Museum)

and should it be decided to put the airplane in production, large savings in time would be accomplished by taking action now . . . Mr. McDonnell wanted approval to go ahead full blast with the necessary engineering to make the second airplane a production prototype including two designs for a limited production quantity with the understanding that if the performance figures of the first airplane turned out to be sour, the whole program would be cancelled. He estimated that an additional $250,000 would be spent by going ahead with the proposed program within the next three months."

Officially recorded statements that "the engine has performed satisfactorily" in tests and that in those tests "engine difficulties were practically non-existant [sic]" should be borne in mind when encountering comments about the XP-67 program being doomed from the start due to the use of unreliable fire-prone engines.

A handwritten note at the bottom of that IOM is extremely interesting: "[General] Carroll proposes – (1) select best available engine for No 2 airplane; (2) if the second a/c is a success, go into production." In early 1944, production of a P-67 of some sort was still being seriously considered.

McDonnell's proposals were certainly ambitious and aggressive, but lurking within the USAAF's response was the belief that the I-1430 situation made it unnecessary to do any further work on the second prototype XP-67. When work was stopped on Ship Two, it left that prototype only 15 percent complete. If things should go wrong in the flight test program, it would be unavailable to back up Ship One without much delay and a great deal of additional money. That would turn out to have catastrophic consequences in the long run.

In the meantime, repairs were made at Scott Field to the damage suffered on the first flight. The rear sections of the nacelles were cut back as recommended, leaving the turbosupercharger flight hood and waste gate tailpipe fully exposed. Judging from the limited photographic evidence available, it was probably at this time that additional venting was also provided for the aft end of each nacelle.

Aft ends of nacelles were cut back and more vents were installed in the rear sections of each nacelle to address initial flight test overheating problems. (Gerald Balzer Collection, Greater St Louis Air and Space Museum)

Because it was feared that the engines themselves might have been damaged by the thermal events in the first flight, out of an abundance of caution it was desired to replace them with backup engines from Continental. The XP-67's Case History report implies that this was

Added between first flight (1/6/1944) and second flight (1/26/1944)

1. Cooling air inlet aft of nozzle box firewall
2. Upper nacelle air exit forward of nozzle box firewall
3. Lower nacelle air exit forward of nozzle box firewall

XP-67 COCKPIT

Instrument panels:

1. Altimeter
2. Airspeed indicator
3. Temperatures (selectable thermocouple source)
4. Unidentified equipment, possibly gunsight
5. Breathing oxygen valve
6. Carburetor air temperature
7. Left engine torquemeter
8. Right engine torquemeter
9. Magnesyn compass (direction indicator)
10. Compass (directional gyroscope)
11. Clock
12. Artificial horizon (attitude indicator)
13. Fuel pressure
14. Thermocouple selector switch
15. Data recording control box
16. Ammeter

17. Ammeter
18. Left turbosupercharger tachometer
19. Right turbosupercharger tachometer
20. Turn and bank indicator
21. Vertical speed indicator
22. Left and right engine tachometer
23. Left and right engine manifold pressure
24. Fuel quantity
25. Accelerometer
26. Left and right turbosupercharger manifold pressure
27. Flaps and landing gear position
28. Left and right engine coolant temperature
29. Left and right engine oil temperature

30. Left and right engine oil pressure
31. Suction
32. Synchronizer RPM control
33. Magneto/ignition switches
34. Right engine fuel selector
35. Left engine fuel selector
36. Starter energizing and mesh switches
37. Fuel booster pump high–low selector
38. Synchronizer tachometer
39. Hydraulic pressure
40. Emergency brake reservoir pressure
41. Recording control box

Controls:

42. Column and yoke
43. Rudder pedals
44. Microphone switch
45. Throttles

46. Mixture controls
47. Quadrant friction control
48. Propeller controls
49. Turbosupercharger intercooler shutter control
50. Test instrumentation
51. Three-axis trim tab controls
52. Switch/fuse panel
53. Left fire extinguisher control
54. Right fire extinguisher control
55. Recognition light controls
56. Radio SCR-274N remote control BC-450
57. SCR-274N control box BC-451
58. Test instrumentation
59. Radio crystal filter selector
60. Emergency landing gear handle
61. Emergency hydraulic pump
62. Chute release handles

The number, type, and location of cockpit components varied quite a bit in the XP-67's short life. The addition of more and more items led to the fitment of an upper panel, which then had one of its six instruments moved up and over to make room for an oddly located breathing oxygen bottle as well as an unidentified piece of equipment believed to be related to a planned gunsight installation. Meanwhile, USAAF pilots' comments after flying the aircraft were critical of control and instrument layout, so significant changes were made there as well. By the end of the summer of 1944, the cockpit looked like this.

done, but the Final Report makes no mention of it, nor does any of the surviving contemporary correspondence. Continental's engine disposition records are murky at best and it is impossible to say for sure whether or not such a change took place.

Regardless, flights two and three then went well, but on February 1, 1944, things went wrong again with flight four. McDonnell himself received a phone call afterward from Capt Aldridge to discuss what had happened, and a transcript of their conversation still exists, thanks to a request that the St Louis Area Office had made to MAC to record all calls from Aldridge's unit. The most significant part was this, with things that are blurred or faded in the microfilm copy indicated in brackets:

A[ldridge]: Well, Mr. Mac, I wonder if you would bring me up to date on this little engine trouble we had the other day?
M[cDonnell]: Yes sir. At about 1 p.m. on February 1, the plane took off and –
A: Excuse me, was that the fourth flight?
M: Let's see, the first flight was January 6 and the next flight was about January 26 – yes, this was the fourth flight. The third flight was the long flight of about 67 minutes. One hour and seven minutes.
A: Yes sir. I remember you saying, Mr. Mac, that that flight had taken place.
M: Right. Now this was the fourth flight at about 1 p.m. on February 1 and while over the runway on the take-off, the photographic record showed that the left engine went up to [3,770? 3,990?] r.p.m. at a manifold pressure of [illegible].
A: That was the left engine again?
M: Yes sir. It likewise showed that at [3,450? 3,650?] r.p.m. at a manifold pressure of 72, the main center bearing burned out. On the right engine the tachometer broke and so we have no record of what it did as regards r.p.m. Now about 200 yards beyond the end of the runway at an altitude of about [50] feet, the canopy came off – the [cockpit canopy]. We were very fortunate that it didn't hit anything on the airplane [??], after having been in the air only [?? minutes].
[Skip to next relevant section of text]
M: [Now] when he landed, the canopy lock lever was in the unlocked position. The pilot [stated] that prior to the take-off, he had locked it. We now have a card with all the operations to be performed prior to take-off which is repeated over the [radio] prior to the takeoff to the pilot and he checks back. The cockpit canopy lock is an item that was not on that card and I have instructed our Chief Engineer that it will be on the card from now on. The pilot, however, after giving it due thought, is positive that he locked the cockpit canopy. [Our examination] of the canopy and of the cockpit [shows] none of the [mechanism failed]. I mean no pins were sheared, and we are going to set the canopy up and put it under an up load

and some vibration and see if, in that way, we can open it up. From the drawings, our engineers don't see how it could open up by itself but on the other hand, it actually came off so we will make that check to see if there is some element involved there that will permit up load and vibration to take it off. Now as regards additional things, we need two additional engines. As of about a week ago, we had put in a requisition for two stand-by engines, through Army channels, and so that [??] is on its way so far as we know. Now Continental – after this engine failure we contacted Continental and they said it would be at least nine days before those two stand-by engines could be here. We feel we shouldn't take a chance on the right engine but that it should go back to the factory to have a look at its main center bearing too. Now in view of that hold-up of nine days in any case, we have taken the plane back to Lambert Field and are putting on the [3C] lips and several other things that we've been holding up until sometime when the ship would be laid up anyway.
A: Good.

Months later, it would be theorized by Col Bogert of the Engineering Division's Technical Staff that the overspeeding of the engines might have been due to "improper setting of the prop synchronizer or failure of the propeller governors to govern properly," which seem like reasonable ideas that would explain the immediacy of the event after takeoff. These marked the first actual failure of an engine in the program, and even then, the failure was not caused by failures in the engines themselves.

Needing new engines, the aircraft returned to St Louis. It would do the rest of its flight testing out of Lambert Field. Continental informed MAC that it would need some time to deliver the engines, and so an opportunity fortuitously presented itself to make a series of upgrades to the aircraft.

By this time the lessons of the wind tunnel were clear. The XP-67 needed to make changes to its engine inlet duct design in order to increase cooling, improve pressure recovery, and reduce ram drag. The way those inlets were faired into the nacelles and wings would also need revision, particularly to the outboard sections. Longitudinal stability needed to be enhanced by raising the horizontal tail 12in., which at

Inlets evolved significantly over time. The February–March rebuild also resulted in a major resculpting of the nacelle contours. (Gerald Balzer Collection, Greater St Louis Air and Space Museum)

the same time would raise the vertical tail by the same amount. Other changes included the addition of a cylindrical piece of equipment above the main instrument panel that required reworking of the upper panel to fit, and the appearance of a small aperture in the tip of the nose cone as well as a very small hole in the inboard section of the wing adjacent to the fuselage. Cuffs were also fitted to the propeller blades at this time.

The inlet duct revisions, in particular, made a noticeable difference to the appearance of the aircraft from the front. Gone were the swoopy fluid curves, replaced with much more utilitarian-looking designs. Small additional scoops appeared for specific air feeds, and the outboard parts of the nacelles that once flowed in smooth curves into the wing leading edge became almost slab-sided by comparison, all in the name of reduced drag from wind-tunnel results ("Revision 3-C, 3-D, and 3-E" as shown earlier in the NACA report drawing). This is what McDonnell meant when he told Aldridge that they were "putting on the 3C lips" in St Louis.

On March 23, 1944, the XP-67 returned to the air, making two flights that day. We know what happened on those flights, thanks to a preserved record of a telephone call from Covington at MAC to the recently promoted Maj Aldridge. The first flight was 15–20 minutes long, cut short because the landing gear doors were not completely shut and they needed to be adjusted on the ground. The second flight, about half-an-hour in duration, was a turbo test run at 10,000ft but one of the turbos failed to work, ground inspection failing to determine what caused the problem. Aldridge suggested that they "give it another whirl" and see if the failure recurred, but the more interesting result from this particular flight was that, in Covington's words, "we made a change in the aileron system to reduce loads on the ailerons and the loads are down now to the point where Ed [Elliott] considers them satisfactory. The ratio of aileron loads to elevator loads is very good. When he landed it yesterday he thinks the landing speed was 103. However, I think that was optimistic. We have not developed our film to see whether that is right." Aldridge responded that "[h]e reported 117 last time," to which Covington replied, "[t]hat was his report but it is hard to judge when landing and we will have to develop the film and see what it was." As far as we know, none of those films have survived, and landing speed numbers do not appear subsequently in any documentation that has been found, including the Final Report.

Aldridge then began pushing for an early follow-up flight in order to get some badly needed data on speed. That was one of the key performance guarantees made in the S-23A Specification, and it was probably the single most important data point that the Army was interested in, in evaluating how well the XP-67 might function in its intended role. Unfortunately, Covington seemed reluctant to pursue the data. "Speed won't mean anything," he responded, citing a need to reduce drag on the airplane; "we have to clean the scoops off" and take out the parachute (it's not known exactly what was meant by this, since the XP-67 is not known to have ever been fitted with a spin chute)

The outboard nacelles required extensive local changes to underlying structure, with the original configuration shown in the top image and the "3-C" changes at the bottom. (Gerald Balzer Collection, Greater St Louis Air and Space Museum)

"and a few things like that. It really won't mean anything," until the airplane was properly prepared. Parts of that section of the transcript are unfortunately illegible, but Covington must have included the "lips" (i.e., the leading-edge inlets) in his list of things to clean up, because Aldridge specifically asks, "[w]hat do you mean by cleaning up the lip?" Covington's reply was surprising, given the trouble that the XP-67 had already experienced with cooling, that had led to careful redesign of the whole air intake system: "I mean the scoops on the airplane. I am sure we . . . are going to be able to take most of them off." Aldridge pushed again for a speed run, and Covington dodged by repeating that "[t]he big thing we are looking for now" was the problem with one of the turbo units.

That conversation also gives a rare glimpse into the aircraft's flying qualities. Covington mentioned that Elliott "was very pleased when he came in yesterday. The airplane is apparently better from a stability standpoint with the tail raised but raising the tail has increased the rudder forces. However, that was without any balancing tab on and last night we hooked up the balancing tab so that should take care of that." Aldridge wrapped up the call by asking to be notified if a flight was to be made that morning, but Covington again demurred, saying that the turbo problem needed to be sorted out first.

At this point, flying seems to have settled down into a routine for the most part, but one event stands out in particular. On April 22, 1944, Brig Gen Carroll sent a letter to McDonnell's Executive Vice President G. W. Carr pointing out a surprising fact that has been conspicuously absent from XP-67 discussions for decades. Emphasis is added in bold by the authors to this extract: "In the telephone conversation it was pointed out by Mr. Hineman [McDonnell's chief liaison engineer, and one of three project managers] that **it was not possible to obtain coolant temperatures in flight on the XP-67**

airplane of great enough magnitude for satisfactory operation of the engine. This, Mr. Hineman explained, was due to the fact that the landing gear [illegible] doors were used as one side of the duct which supplies cooling air to the radiator. It was further explained when these doors were closed tightly that the flow of air through the cooling air duct to the radiator was governed by an exit flap but since these doors would not close tightly, **in normal flight and in the case of landing procedure when the doors were completely open, the exit flap has little or no control over the cooling flow and results in extremely low temperatures in the cooling system.** This condition is definitely very unsatisfactory and cannot be tolerated on any airplane accepted by the Army Air Forces. However, Mr. Hineman pointed out that a satisfactory fix on the airplane which is not flying is next to the impossible and requested that the company be allowed, as a fix for this airplane only, to incorporate upon the coolant radiator a thermostatic by-pass valve similar to those used in the oil temperature regulators of [standard] installations. The use of such a system is undesirable for this type airplane inasmuch as **a thermostatic by-pass merely limits the amount of coolant [flow] through the radiator whereas the cooling air flow is at all times a maximum providing a maximum pumping loss for cooling air as well as a maximum drag loss**, while the actual cooling afforded the engine cooling system will be entirely dependent upon the coolant flow through the radiator."

So rather than operating in a chronically overheated condition, the engines were actually being run at undesirably cool temperatures. The temporary solution, a thermostatic bypass, may or may not have resolved the problem in this particular case; no specific information relating to that has been found. The side effect of such a makeshift fix was a "maximum drag loss," the very thing that the inlet duct redesign had been developed to prevent. This raises a serious problem that should be kept in mind when interpreting the XP-67's performance relative to guarantees. A major drag increase that would not have been present when the system was correctly redesigned for service use would mean that the performance of the XP-67 would always be lower than a production-configured aircraft would have been.

Brig Gen Carroll summed it up briefly: "After consideration of the possibilities and due to the impossibility of providing a satisfactory fix to the present airplane, it was decided that a by-pass system incorporating a thermostatic valve may be used on the one airplane now flying. This type system is not to be used on any other airplane supplied by McDonnell Aircraft to the Army Air Forces. Any airplanes designed or in the process of fabrication at the McDonnell Aircraft plant should be reworked to provide an independent air duct for radiator cooling air and the cooling air flow shall be controlled by an automatic exit flap." If nothing else, the XP-67 program at least provided this "lesson learned" for future designs at MAC.

In any event, test flying continued with Ed Elliott at the controls. A Progress Report has been found that summarizes a key period beginning on May 1, 1944:

A variety of changes, major and minor, were made to the XP-67 between its roll-out and final flight. Most of its flight testing, between March and late summer 1944, was done in this configuration. During that time, details changed. For example, the air scoops on the right engine nacelle were modified slightly in contour from the corresponding ones on the left nacelle, and for unknown reasons seem to have never been painted. Various forms of the white striping on the fuselage nose and tail are recorded in photographs of the period, as are remnants of the yellow striping on the wings. A small glass aperture appeared at the tip of the nose cone. In late summer 1944, most of the cooling vents and scoops that had been added were removed to reduce drag in preparation for the upcoming all-important high-speed demonstration flights, but very few flights were accomplished in that configuration.

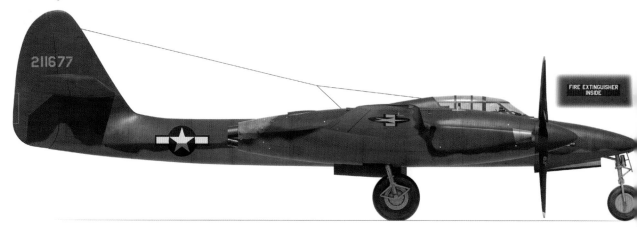

Flights:

May 1, 1944 – 40 minutes.

May 4, 1944 – 53 minutes "with good results and was reported best flight made to date, but continued engine roughness."

May 5, 1944 – 18 minutes.

May 5, 1944 – second flight of the day, 17 minutes "with good results."

At this point, the USAAF took over briefly with three of its own highly experienced pilots: Col M. F. Cooper, Lt Col O. J. Ritland, and Maj F. A. Borsodi. The Progress Report gives a top-level summary of their activities:

May 11, 1944 – Wright Field pilots arrive. Col Cooper flies 35 minutes, Lt Col Ritland flies 45 minutes, revealing damaged LH prop tips; replacement made.

May 12, 1944 – Maj Borsodi flies 40 minutes; hydraulic line failure at RH engine, but "emergency system functioned satisfactorily and necessary repairs were made."

May 13, 1944 – Col Cooper flies 55 minutes with Lt Col Ritland pacing in P-51B.

May 13, 1944 – second flight of the day, Lt Col Ritland flies 35 minutes.

Following these flights, a report was written to record their observations and impressions. Principal findings documented in the Pilots' Comments report were as follows, with authors' notes in brackets:

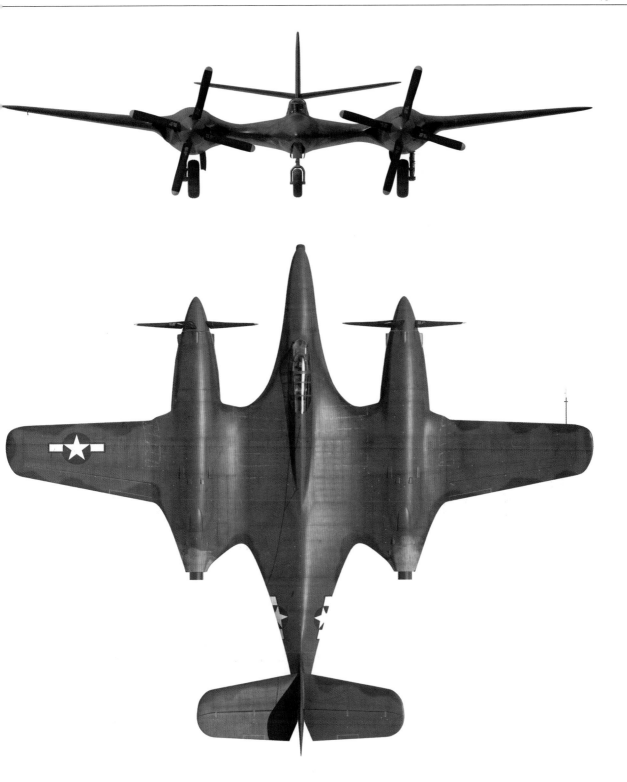

McDONNELL XP-67 42-11677, LAMBERT FIELD, MISSOURI, SPRING 1944

– "The take-off run is unusually long and gives the pilot the sensation that the airplane is under powered . . . Initial climb is poor and immediately after take-off forward vision is considerably restricted." Also: "After take-off the acceleration to minimum safe single engine speed is slow."

– "The rate of climb is low at all altitudes for fighter type airplanes."

– "At 22,000 ft. the airplane begins to feel mushy and response to controls is slow."

– "Cooling during all climbs was good."

– "All controls are effective from high speeds to the stall except the elevators may be blanketed out at high angles of attack near stalling speeds. The rudder becomes somewhat ineffective at slow speed with the gear and flaps extended but aileron control is good throughout the stall."

– "Elevator forces are too light at all speeds."

– "Rate of roll seems good at high speeds."

– ". . . the airplane appeared to be longitudinally stable when the nose was displaced from a trimmed level flight attitude. The resulting oscillations took an excessively long time to dampen out."

– "Laterally the airplane is neutrally stable bordering on divergence."

– "The airplane's directional stability is poor. The damping is slow and the airplane has a peculiar 'swim' or 'Dutch roll' during the oscillations . . . It is felt that the airplane would not be a good gun platform with its present handling characteristics."

– "Elevator and aileron trim controls seemed too sensitive."

– "The engines are very quiet and the noise level is low."

– "The airplane is fairly comfortable, although the rudder pedals are too far apart and the control column is too high. This position would be fatiguing for extended periods of flight."

– "The general vision of the airplane is considered very poor."

– "The ship lands easily although the speed is high (about 120 MPH at contact)." [This suggests that despite the high speed, the unusual wing/fuselage/nacelle layout, which was designed to make everything contribute to lift, was doing its job very well.]

– "Engine cooling was very good for ground operation and all flight conditions, however, the engines cooled very rapidly in low power dives and power off stalls." [This is consistent with Brig Gen Carroll's letter of April 22, 1944 on overcooling.]

– "Flight test performance data was not obtained; however, speed checks were made against a calibrated P-51B at 10,000 ft. and 22,000 ft. pressure altitude at military power (72" hg. at 3200 RPM or 280 lb. torque pressure). At 22,000 ft. the maximum level speed was 272 MPH IAS which corrected to approximately 393 MPH true. The 10,000 ft. run at the same power corrected to approximately 357 MPH true airspeed."

After this mix of good and bad features came a somber Conclusions section:

The other major visual change coming out of the February–March 1944 rebuild involved the tail section. The original height of the tail is seen on the left, and the 12in. vertical extension added on the right, conveniently marked with the date. (Gerald Balzer Collection, Greater St Louis Air and Space Museum)

"1. The performance of the airplane was not good in comparison to present fighters particularly in rate of climb, take-off and landing characteristics and service and combat ceiling.

"2. The flying characteristics in respect to stability and maneuverability leave much to be desired. Visibility is poor for all conditions of flight. The cockpit layout could be improved with but few changes.

"3. The airplane is not considered safe for the average military pilot with its present high landing speed and long take-off run. [A different propeller might have cured this, and in fact dual-rotation props were desired by McDonnell and even approved by Col Bogert on May 30, 1944, but were not installed. Even a different single prop might have been better for takeoffs and landings, but at the risk of further compromising an already unimpressive high-speed capability. But a critical unanswered, in fact apparently unasked, question was: What would dual-rotation props do to stability? It had already been found that the aircraft was unstable for all cases where the props rotated down on the near-fuselage side, and that is why they were arranged to rotate up on that side. Dual-rotation props would reduce whatever prop slipstream effects were occurring, both bad and good; would they have reduced, or eliminated, or even reversed the stability margin that the XP-67's original props were providing? Regarding the "high landing speed," the only numbers that have survived are from the telephone conversation between Covington and Aldridge, where 103–117mph are mentioned. North American Aviation's Report NA-46-130 for the P-51D lists its landing speed as 110.7mph, in the same ballpark. The P-38 Pilot's Manual, meanwhile, says to "come over the fence at 110 mph." B-26s in combat squadrons were making landings at 114mph every day. XP-67's landing speed certainly did not keep it from meeting its landing requirement either; in fact it bettered it, with more than 100ft shorter distance than specified. As for takeoff distance, the original S-23 Specification for the XP-67 required 2,853ft and the Final Report shows that it was just 165ft (5.8 percent) more than that. These numbers make it hard to understand the "not considered safe" remark.]

"4. With its present poor rate of climb, the only tactical mission for which this airplane appears to be suitable is that of a long range escort fighter. If used for such missions, the increased fuel load required would raise the gross weight to over 25,000 lbs. with a corresponding effect on the already poor climb and take-off. With improved visibility the airplane could be used for ground support missions." [In January 1943, Brig Gen Carroll had responded to a McDonnell idea for an "A-67" attack variant using Allison engines. Unlike what service pilots would later note, forecasting suggested that "the forward visibility is exceptionally attractive. This is a very important aspect in attack airplanes." Reality apparently showed otherwise.]

The report finishes with "Recommendations: None."

While the report itself was discouraging, a July 18, 1944, message from Brig Gen M. E. Gross of the Requirements Division, Assistant Chief of the Air Staff, Operations, Commitments, & Requirements (AC/AS OC&R), Washington DC, to Assistant Chief of the Air Staff, Materiel, Maintenance and Distribution (AC/AS, MM&D), Washington DC, painted an almost completely different picture. The poor take-off quality of the XP-67 was acknowledged, but otherwise, "the general flight handling characteristics of the airplane are delightful. It handles exceptionally well, has beautiful stall characteristics, and the roll characteristics are good, although the control forces are high." It is difficult to reconcile these comments with those made by Ritland, Borsodi, and Cooper.

In between the Pilots' Comments report and the July 18 message, there was another item regarding the subjects of performance and flying qualities. On June 27, 1944, R. H. Miller, chief aerodynamics engineer, and W. J. Blatz, testing, from McDonnell met with Lawrence A. Clousing and William M. Kauffman of the Flight Research Section at Moffett Field, California, and "discussed certain XP-67 handling qualities problems," apparently prompted by what the three USAAF pilots had said. According to a memorandum dated June 30, 1944, "Mr. Miller stated . . . that as modified at present, the airplane appeared to possess satisfactory flying qualities, except for low rates of roll and a long-period control-free lateral oscillation." These matters were discussed in detail, and it appeared that the solution to the low rate of roll would be simple – a preloaded aileron spring tab system – while the lateral oscillation was outside of the USAAF's requirements to begin with, and only appeared when the pilot was flying hands-off, not when his hands were on the controls. It was thought by the Flight Research Section experts that this might actually be caused by a "hunting" effect between slightly-out-of-synch left and right engines. If so, then it was not an inherent characteristic of the aircraft itself.

To sum up, the Pilots' Comments report describes the XP-67's handling qualities differently than other documents, and it is hard to resolve some of the discrepancies. For example, immediately after the first flight, Aldridge told his superiors that "the pilot reported that the ship handled very nicely and a landing was effected without difficulty, although at a rather high speed." But the Case History cites an Inter-Desk Memorandum from Col M. C. Demler, OAC/AS, MM&D, to Col J. F. Phillips, also OAC/AS, which said that the landing speed and roll were shorter than anticipated, not faster and longer. It does agree that the aircraft handled very well. As mentioned earlier, Covington had passed along Elliott's observation to Aldridge about the aircraft's stability and handling being improved by the major changes incorporated in February and March 1944, which established the configuration in which Cooper, Ritland, and Borsodi flew the aircraft. The XP-67 Case History report sums up the USAAF pilots' comments as "the general opinion seemed to be that the XP-67 airplane 'is under-powered but performs quite well.'"

In viewing all of this in context, it must be remembered that the three USAAF pilots made a total of just five flights between them (Cooper twice, total 90 minutes; Ritland twice, total 80 minutes; Borsodi once, 40 minutes). It is hard to imagine that this was enough time for any of them to truly get the feel of the aircraft or become comfortable with its controls and display layout. In the end, though, it is possible to select passages from the record to support any rating of flying qualities. The only person who flew the aircraft long enough to be thoroughly familiar with its characteristics was Ed Elliott, and there is no direct record of his thoughts on the subject. His son, Marc Elliott, however, told the authors that "he always said that he loved that airplane." That's probably as close as it is possible to come to a final authoritative word on the subject.

Not long after the USAAF pilot flights, allegations were apparently being raised again about persistent engine problems, parts coming off of the aircraft while flying, and very long intervals between flights. Col H. Z. Bogert, Chief of Technical Staff, Engineering Division, responded formally regarding this to Maj Aldridge in a letter dated June 20, 1944: "In regard to fires in the airplane and cowling coming off at high speeds, this has not occurred since the first four flights which were made last winter. On the first flight there were fires in the turbo compartments due to exhaust gases from the turbo hood entering the turbo compartment, and on the fourth flight over speeding of the engines occurred due either to improper setting of the prop synchronizer or failure of the propeller governors to govern properly; and during this

NEXT PAGES

Defending Italy from Me 262

A less-delayed development schedule for XP-67 coupled with the possibility that the European war could have lasted far longer with better tactical and strategic decision-making by the Germans could have seen the P-67C fighter fielded in time to take part in the air war. Germany had planned to send two squadrons of Me 262A-2A fighter-bombers to Italy by June 1945. Their top speed of 470mph when laden with external bombs would have been a severe problem for the P-38s being used as interceptors there, but McDonnell was estimating the P-67C's jet-boosted top speed to be 502mph at sea level, 560mph at 18,500ft, and 559mph at 32,000ft, making it well capable of dealing with the Messerschmitts. Here, a P-67C of the 97th Fighter Squadron, 82nd Fighter Group in Italy (formerly a P-38 unit) has taken one of the German jets by surprise from behind, while another P-67C is curving in for a frontal attack if one should prove necessary.

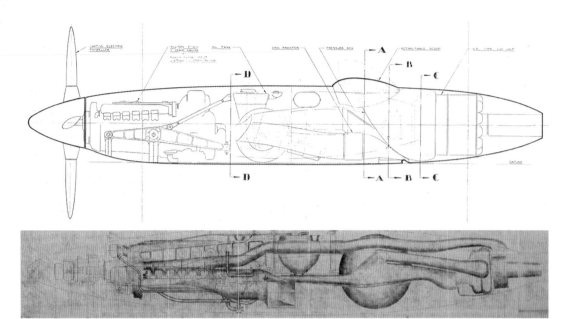

flight, which was only of a five minutes duration, the pilot's canopy came off. Following the fourth flight which took place on 4 February 1944, the airplane was laid up for approximately six weeks for modification of the leading edge duct entrances and raising of the horizontal tail. The fifth flight occurred on 25 March 1944. Approximately fifty flights have been accomplished and no serious functional difficulties have been encountered. This is an average of better than one flight every two days rather than one flight every two weeks to a month."

Hopefully, this will stand as the definitive word on the still-commonly held beliefs about the XP-67 being doomed by a substandard engine.

It was just at this point that the issue of powerplants for service variants resurfaced. Absent the I-1430 engine, which would never see production, and given the desire for higher speeds, MAC had conceptualized mixed-propulsion piston/jet configurations, as described earlier. A variety of layouts were sketched, using Allison or Rolls-Royce 14SM engines, single or dual-rotation propellers, and General Electric I-20 or 9½in. diameter Westinghouse jet engines in the rear. Only two of the sketches are known to survive, but they show radically different packagings of the piston and jet engines.

Earlier in 1944, MAC had asked for, and received, permission to install dual-rotation (counterrotating) propellers on XP-67 Ship One as a means of getting the war emergency rated power of the engines at an early date. Official performance tests were to be done with single-rotation propellers at military ratings, then dual propellers would be installed and provisions would be added for water injection. Performance runs would then be flown with the dual propellers and water injection. Part of this plan was to continue building Ship Two, which would not be affected by the contemplated change in engines despite an earlier informal agreement to stop construction altogether pending Ship One findings. Incorporating the modifications needed

Two of the MAC mixed-propulsion concepts whose sketches have survived. The lower sketch seems to show a vague XP-67 influence in the region of the piston engine supports, but basically either of these would have needed totally new nacelles. (Gerald Balzer Collection, Greater St Louis Air and Space Museum, top, and Ron Farver Collection, below)

for that engine change would be approved contingent on success with Ship One's flight testing.

One of those tasked with reviewing these concepts as well as the XP-67 itself was Col M. S. Roth of the Engineering Division at Wright Field, who, in a July 14, 1944 telephone conversation with Col R. C. Wilson, Chief of Development Engineering, was asked directly, "[w]hat are you all going to do with the XP-67?" Roth's reply, and in fact the entire subsequent conversation, revealed extreme negativity about MAC and its new aircraft: "We think they are running into too much money . . . I can't see going on with McDonnell myself. I was willing to drop the project some time ago."

At one point Roth made a very interesting observation: "That airplane makes the runway look awfully short. There is something wrong with the propeller; it is not pulling out the maximum horsepower of the engines by torque meter reading. It does not seem to get going. An airplane of that weight and power should get going and get off much quicker, although the wing loading is pretty high." This is a strong hint that the XP-67's small propellers relative to the similarly powered Lockheed XP-49 may in fact have been the root cause of the performance problems. Ground clearance limitations would have prevented the fitting of propellers as large as the XP-49's without lengthening the XP-67's landing gear, which would require major redesign of the engine nacelles into which they retracted. Unlike other aircraft, those nacelles were smoothly faired into the wing surfaces, so redesign of the latter would also have been required. So while its performance may well have been improved with larger propellers, they were never a realistic option for the XP-67. This whole subject was well understood by Roth, as the conversation would go on to prove.

Wilson asked whether there would be Continental engines, and strangely, given that this possibility had been eliminated some time ago, Roth replied yes. The discussion then swung around to hybrid propulsion, with Roth saying, "McDonnell has been in here several times selling the idea of installing the Rolls-Royce engine with the I-70 in back but has not been back since I told him he ought to wait and see if he has a flying machine in the one he now has." Wilson agreed: "That ought to be our attitude, I think."

Roth seemed to have a realistic grasp of what the mixed-propulsion concept would actually involve, as opposed to marketing charts and notional layout drawings: "[McDonnell's] conversation will lead you to believe that all there is to it is a couple of new engines and the I-70 [sic] in back but it is not that. It is a complete new airplane. The nacelles will have to be changed, and an extra wing panel added, raise the pilot's cockpit, added span, need a new tail, etc. The peculiar shape of that airplane requires everything to be faired in from one thing to another which when put all together means a complete new airplane." In a strange way, at least part of this was due to inputs to Continental from the USAAF the previous year, when Roth, himself, took part in a review of the draft powerplant engineering drawings for a -21 variant of the engine. The records of that meeting show that "Colonel Roth stated that it was highly desirable to keep the height of the engine at the rear to a minimum value so as to permit cowling the engine quite closely in high speed fighter aircraft. [Continental's] Mr. Kinnucan stated that the suggestions obtained from the Materiel Center representatives in respect to these matters would be given full consideration." Although not specific to the XP-67, Roth's remarks are certainly consistent with the tight packing of the engine and its ductwork in MAC's aircraft, which led to the unfeasibility of making the switch to a larger engine without requiring major structural redesign.

At the end of his conversation with Wilson, Roth seemed to slam the door on any future USAAF operational role: "I don't think we will get anything out of it. That is my personal opinion. I think we ought to fly this one to see if anything is in the aerodynamic shape. That is what we want to know." Wilson agreed, and the next day he sent a communication directly to Brig Gen Gross outlining the problems and stating that "Materiel Command desires to complete the test on No. 1 airplane before considering any further development of this airplane." In other words, until and unless the sole flying XP-67 proved that it could deliver the performance required in the S-23A specification, there should be no mixed-propulsion derivatives, no alternative-mission configurations, and no Service variants at all.

On July 18, 1944, Brig Gen Gross responded with a bit of push-back, praising the XP-67's flight and handling qualities, as mentioned above. He also noted that the airframe had the potential to install a .60cal gun, that was being worked on, more so than other aircraft under development. This, he thought, would make a P-67 service aircraft of great interest for the long-range strike and ground-strafing roles. Gross agreed that the XP-67 needed to complete its testing, but reaffirmed that "it appears to be an airplane whose possibilities should be fully explored."

On the same day as his message to Brig Gen Gross, Col Wilson sent out another to specifically quash the idea of a photo-reconnaissance variant of the P-67. Five reasons were given: flight characteristics that did not meet those required for a photographic aircraft; serious camera cut-off due to nacelles and camera mounting locations that would prevent suitable mapping coverage; too slow at sea level for tactical reconnaissance; worries about the turbulence likely to be created when placing flat optical glass panels in the smoothly blended moldline; and worse pilot visibility, service ceiling, rate of climb, and maneuverability than the existing F-5 aircraft.

Numerous small vents and exhausts were eliminated during the July–August 1944 major rework cycle. (Gerald Balzer Collection, Greater St Louis Air and Space Museum)

Before July-August 1944

After July-August 1944

The common thread in all of this was that there was an urgent need to finish the scheduled XP-67 flight test program and quantify its performance. Unfortunately, just at this time the aircraft had to be taken out of service after its July 3, 1944, flight for "extensive rework and repairs" that would keep it from flying again until August 24. The Final Report strangely fails to mention this break, saying that "flight testing continued throughout the summer of 1944," although clearly this was not the case. It also notes that the lateral stability issues were still being investigated, and potential fixes were being explored, such as wires on the trailing edge of the rudder, a dorsal fin, and an increase in wing dihedral from 5° to 7°, which seems like a drastic change to make without wind-tunnel data support. Although documentation on the dihedral change is sketchy, it seems that shims and brackets were inserted into the existing structure rather than remanufacturing the entire carry-through structure to the new angles. No photographs have been found that illustrate any of these changes.

Meanwhile, I-1430 testing at Continental had already demonstrated 50 hours running at 2,000hp with water injection at war emergency rating. It had been found that with the extremely high-octane 150 grade fuel that was starting to come into service, the engine could provide an even higher war emergency rating of 2,100hp without the use of water injection. Studies by both MAC and Materiel Command found that this power could be handled by an 11ft diameter single-rotation Aeroproducts propeller blade design H-20-156. Although still a foot-and-a-half less in diameter and having a 23 percent smaller disk area the propeller fitted to the XP-49, it was about as big a propeller as could be squeezed in while preserving at least minimal ground clearance. In any event, the plans for dual-rotation propellers were canceled, but the Aeroproducts propellers were never installed either, and the XP-67 flew to the end with its original 10ft 6in. diameter Curtiss C5425 propellers.

The Final Report gave a brief summary of other changes: "The contractor's flight tests during the summer also included a drag reduction program which involved smoother fairings, elimination of extraneous air scoops, etc." This represents the fulfillment of Covington's comment on things to be changed before doing a speed run, in his March telephone conversation with Aldridge: "we have to clean the scoops off."

In its description of events in the summer of 1944, the Final Report mentions something that does not appear in the Case History or any other known surviving documentation: "During this period, the airplane was flown by several more Army Air Force pilots including Colonel M.S. Roth." No other contemporary source mentions this, or gives any details on exactly when this took place, or even who the other pilots were, so it is not possible to know whether Roth's strong negativity about the XP-67 was formed before or after he had actually flown it.

Of less import but intriguing nonetheless, it was also at this time that significant changes were made to at least the upper instrument panel (the row of six gauges above the main panel). One of the center gauges was bumped up to sit over the one to its left, and a cutout was made where it had been in the panel, to make room for a large knob and linkage at the end of what appears to have been an oxygen tank for the pilot. Why this odd location was selected, and where the bottle had been prior to this, are not recorded.

While all of this was going on, the technical staff had not been idle. A test program had been forwarded to the chief of the Flight Section at Wright Field on August 29, 1944, outlining the data that would be collected "sometime near the forepart of September," or in other words, almost immediately. It mentions that two "photopanels" were installed in the XP-67 and that "Flight Section instruments pertaining to performance" would be mounted there, as well as "any McDonnell instrumentation pertaining to airplane, engine, and turbo operation." A variety of level flight tests were to be flown: power calibration at 5,000ft, 25,000ft, and 30,000ft. The middle altitude case would be flown through as great a power range as possible to obtain speed and power data, which would be combined with fuel consumption data to enable calculations of range. Possibly of most importance in the minds of the USAAF customers, single-point high-speed runs would be made at military power at three altitudes: 15,000ft, 20,000ft, and 27,000ft. These would be used to generate the standard speed-versus-altitude curve for military power or limiting rpm, whichever was most restrictive at each altitude. That data would be reduced to standard manifold pressure of 72in. mercury up to critical altitude, and to 24,800 turbo rpm above that. The test program document contains generic sketches of the specific graphs that would be created.

Climb tests were also covered. The plan specified "sawtooth" climbs to be flown from 8,000–11,000ft and from 27,000–28,500ft to quantify the best climb speed that the aircraft could achieve. Melding the climb and level flight tests, as the aircraft was heading to one of the high-altitude speed-power points a short climb was to be made at the best climbing speed shown by the lower sawtooth test, to determine the critical altitude in climb, so that one point would be obtained regarding best climbing speed above that altitude. Other climbs would be done at military power to determine service and absolute ceiling at that power, and if time was available, check climbs would also be flown at normal rated power. Again, sample graphs were provided to show the expected data that would be obtained. The same engine operating conditions were to be observed as in the level flight tests.

Another series of tests would have shown how fuel efficient the XP-67 was. At 25,000ft altitude, the range covered per gallon of fuel used would be determined for engine power settings from 1,800–3,200rpm.

Everything seemed in place to finally come to grips with what the XP-67 could actually do. Ground tests on the reworked aircraft began on August 24, 1944, followed by a five-minute flight on August 28 whose shortness was due to low oil pressure thanks to defective oil seals. More short flights that were made over the next five days turned

Original

Relocated instrument

Final

Forward vision, criticized by USAAF pilots, deteriorated even further with the addition of a cylindrical piece of equipment that intruded into the upper instrument panel, forcing one instrument to be moved to a position above the adjacent one. (Gerald Balzer Collection, Greater St Louis Air and Space Museum; National Museum of the United States Air Force)

up other problems requiring rework and repair. A Progress Report dated September 4, 1944, mentions ground runs of both engines on August 24, followed by removal of their filters for "cleaning and inspection" and removal also of the turbo tail cones for inspection. Another ground check was made, running both engines for 26 minutes, and a taxi test was done.

Two days later, another ground operations checkout was made, followed by a flight to check on directional stability following the increase in wing dihedral, but unfortunately that was not able to be quantitatively established because the flight had to be cut short after just five minutes. It was noted, however, that "especially heavy forces" were needed to move the ailerons, which, said the Progress Report, was "no doubt due to the hoped-for increase of lateral stability as a result of change of dihedral."

The reason for terminating the flight so soon was that oil pressure had dropped from 90psi to 50psi, causing oil temperatures to rise, to 120°C in the case of the left engine. The pilot, Ed Elliott as usual, remarked that the left magnetos on both engines (each engine being equipped with two) were "appreciably rough," although it didn't greatly reduce rpms on either engine. Both torquemeter gauges fluctuated rapidly over a range of 20–30 (units illegible) during the flight. Excessive coolant temperatures were also encountered.

As the oil pressure rose, the automatic engine coolant temperature control was not able to keep up, so the pilot unsuccessfully tried manual controls, and the flight had to be terminated. Afterward, Continental's factory representative provided oversight while the engine's accessory case and crankcase were removed, revealing two defective oil seals on the left engine. These were replaced and a steel washer was installed for greater support. The engine was then repressurized to confirm that the fix had been successful. During the teardown, it was also found that an electrical line to the oil cooler was broken. After all of this was rectified, the engine was given a 30-minute ground check on August 29, with no more problems noted.

A flight had been planned for the next day, but weather prevented it. MAC decided to take advantage of the time by installing new landing gear up-locks, as well as new intake manifold hoses on both engines. New backfire screens were installed on the intake of the right engine only, for unspecified reasons. Another ground check was made to confirm again that the engines were operating properly. The Progress Report also notes that work was being done on "filling in low spots on skin laps and joints and painting the airplane," all focused on preserving laminar flow over the skin and keeping drag to a minimum.

The weather had cleared up by the next day, allowing a 40-minute flight to be made. Afterwards, the left engine's crankcase cover was again removed for inspection, followed by another repressurization checkout. Microswitches for landing gear door lights were installed, so that they would be on when the doors were closed. Forward strainers and both oil filters – along with oil pressure regulator, oil pressure gauge, and oil temperature gauge – were all checked. Furthermore, all oil lines were checked for restriction. Clearly there were still concerns about the oil pressure and temperature after this flight, and this is borne out by the

fact that on September 1, yet another ground check was made on the left engine "for malfunctioning oil pressure and temperatures."

September 2 saw a new pilot, Woodward "Woody" Burke, making a familiarization flight of an hour and 15 minutes. Burke's background was as colorful and varied as Elliott's, but unfortunately this would be his only day flying the XP-67; a few months later, he would be killed while test flying MAC's first jet fighter for the US Navy, the XFD-1. After landing the XP-67, he reported that the throttle friction device was stuck. This was fixed, and he made a second flight of 55 minutes that same day. During this flight, the propeller warning lights were on at all times and the left engine oil temperature was still unsatisfactory. Both of Burke's flights were made with oil cooler doors open due to the automatic system being out of order.

The September 4 Progress Report concludes with actions that were planned to be taken next: "[C]ontractor is removing the spoiler from trailing edge of rudder and changing aileron unbalance from 3 / 4:1. Also, left engine oil cooler has been replaced, together with

The XP-67 has just landed on fire in this photo, as vehicles and firefighters race in to try to save the aircraft. (US Government source)

The full extent of the damage appears from this angle. Lower skin sections of the left nacelle also burned through, due to the pool of burning fuel underneath the aircraft. Strangely, despite the fire being intense enough to melt aluminum, none of the aircraft's tires have burned or even burst. (Gerald Balzer Collection, Greater St Louis Air and Space Museum)

This is the rocker arm that failed, starting the fire that ended the XP-67 program. (US Government source)

oil temperature thermostat. Contractor has encountered difficulty in keeping sealing strips on landing flaps and landing gear doors." Then, more ominously, "[r]epairs were made to empennage section as it was revealed that bulkhead angles located between horizontal stabilizers contained cracks approximately 1" long, resulting in the buckling of the skin on left and right hand sides on the aft section of fuselage and also the deformation of the bulkhead section." This is the first instance we know of where structural problems in the airframe were found.

After a few more minor matters, the Progress Report concludes by saying: "Contractor will have the airplane ready for flight this afternoon and a flight will be made, weather permitting."

Whether or not that fight was made is not known, but just two days later, on September 6, 1944, exactly eight months after XP-67's first flight, catastrophe struck. At 13.16 hrs, Elliott had taken the aircraft up to 10,000ft when the right engine began to lose power. Abandoning the test, Elliott radioed the Lambert Field control tower to give the distress signal for an emergency landing. The tower responded that the field was clear and to proceed, so Elliott began to reduce altitude. It was not until reaching 3,000ft that the first sign of fire was seen. By the time the XP-67 touched down on runway 24 at 13.37 hrs, the right wheel well was belching flames and smoke. Elliott tried to point the slowing aircraft so that the wind would blow the flames outboard, limiting damage to the right nacelle and outer wing, but the brake on that side failed and the XP-67 pivoted around to exactly the wrong orientation. The wind thus blew the fire over the fuselage and left wing. Elliott escaped unhurt but the aircraft burned out, the fuselage collapsing just behind the wing, despite heroic firefighting efforts by personnel from the Naval Air Station nearby.

The official accident report mentions that the investigating committee, along with Wright Field representatives, inspected the wreckage, finding that the "No. 1 Exhaust Rocker Arm was broken in such a manner that the Rocker Roller and shaft came out of the arm. After this damage took place, No. 1 exhaust valve remained closed. The intake port to No. 1 cylinder was dry and coated with soot . . . indicating that No. 1 cylinder had been firing probably for four minutes (see . . . data from Photo Record Sheets) and exhausting into the inlet manifold."

The report goes on to give more details, saying that "four minutes of operation at 42" of manifold pressure as noted in the data where exhaust flame backs up through the back-fire screen into the intake manifold, was sufficient heat to destroy the back-fire screen. During the time that the back-fire screen remained intact, exhaust gas was being dumped into the intake manifold, diluting the charge and reducing the power." This was the first symptom that Elliot had noticed, a loss of power on the right engine. "At such time as the screen burned through the exhaust flame set fire to the boosted mixture in the intake manifold which fire was confined to the entering half of the manifold (no charring of exterior paint on the other half) and immediately caused complete loss of power in that engine." After a cascading sequence of parts being damaged and failing due to the extreme heat that they were never designed to withstand, "the fire spread to the exterior of the intake manifold, and was probably fed by fuel… Once the fire was outside of the intake manifold, it started to burn residual oil and rubber connections (the fuel and oil hoses were very close at hand) and the conflagration started," or at least became obvious to the pilots.

"This all took place," the report continues, "in the vicinity of 9,500 feet altitude, and the fire apparently got under way at the same time that the engine lost all power. The fire indicator system didn't work immediately," which is a common occurrence with "fire wire"-type heat sensing systems, since they themselves must be heated by the fire up to a set point at which they illuminate a warning light in the cockpit, "and there was no indication of fire until the pilot had reached 3,000 feet, at which time his red lights went on and he noticed smoke coming from the tail pipe."

This was all considered very unusual. Continental had experienced rocker arm failures multiple times during bench testing of the I-1430, but they had never led to fires. Possibly it shut the engines down as soon as the failure happened rather than letting it continue to run in order to see what would happen, but the XP-67's fire sequence involved a chain of effects on components such as fuel and oil lines, whose character and location would have been greatly different for test stand runs. It is worth noting that modern aircraft generally use optical fire sensors that instantly "see" flame and alert the crew or even activate fire extinguishers automatically, catching fires much more quickly and putting them out much more easily than was possible with the XP-67's equipment.

A great deal of flight data was available to support this accident analysis. Investigators reviewed onboard instrumentation that recorded engine parameters every five seconds, and it showed that there had been no failure of fuel or oil lines during the flight, and that pressure in both had been at normal levels the whole time: "Study of the burned engine showed beyond a doubt that intense fire existed in the intake manifold and in the nacelle. There was no evidence of any other malfunction or discrepancy to cause fire other than the failure of the rocker arm." The human element was also considered, but "[t]here was no evidence of gross negligence on the part of any individuals concerned."

Sadly, the fire that engulfed the aircraft would have been much less damaging had the right brake not failed, allowing the considerable crosswind (measured at 22mph just before the flight) to weathercock the XP-67 into the worst possible position. The accident review committee believed that "had there not been right brake failure only comparative minor damage would have resulted," and after repairs, Ship One could have been returned to flight status. The all-important test runs would then have proven once and for all what the aircraft could or could not do.

But with Ship One now beyond repair, the catastrophic consequences of halting construction of Ship Two became apparent. Curtiss-Wright, also at Lambert, had suffered the loss of its own XP-55 Ship One after a brief flying career, but the company had completed other prototypes and was back in the air with only minor delays. Northrop lost its first XP-56, but had a second almost finished and was able to complete flight testing with it. The "Flying Fillet" had no such options available. With Ship One gone, the program was finished.

Still, the end did not come right away. There were still outstanding contract items that MAC was reimbursed for over the subsequent few weeks. The Production Section, Process Division at Wright Field also requested guidance on whether the Engineering Division wanted to have the XP-67 restored and repaired. The letter also mentioned a "finding of fact by the Contracting Officer that McDonnell was not at fault in the actual destruction of this airplane." The Engineering Division responded that action should be taken to terminate the contract and dispose of "the residual equipment." McDonnell was verbally notified of the decision on October 10, 1944, and was authorized to begin dismantling the XP-67's wreckage. Interestingly, in another teletype message on October 23, the Readjustment Division at Wright Field "stated that the contractor had requested the proposed termination," according to the Case History. The Readjustment Division advised that the contract had been terminated the next day, the reason being "Reduced Requirements of Army Air Forces."

NEXT PAGES

Over Mount Fujiyama

Had the war in the Pacific gone on longer, and if the XP-67 program had succeeded sooner in demonstrating the performance required of it, the P-67E photo-reconnaissance variant might well have gone into production and service, where it could have met advanced Japanese interceptor aircraft such as the Kyushu J7W Shinden. MAC pitched a sample mission that had a P-67E variant based in the Marianas Islands flying all the way to Japan's coast in the Kobe/Osaka area, then photographing all of the area between there and Tokyo (passing Mount Fujiyama along the way) before returning to its base. Here, a P-67E of the 8th Photographic Reconnaissance Squadron (replacing the unit's F-5 variant of the P-38) is using both propellers and jet engines as it approaches Tokyo to stay out of range of three Home Defense Shinden interceptors.

On January 31, 1946, Maj Aldridge issued the Final Report, which was filed with the Historical Office. That marked the last action of the XP-67 program.

How likely was it that the specially cleaned-up XP-67 would have met its performance requirements? That question has prompted much debate over the ensuing decades. The Final Report has a few numbers, based on the flights that were actually flown. But even it says those numbers were "based on very sketchy flight test information," which sounds very negative until the reader realizes that "sketchy" in this sense could just as well mean "overly conservative" as "overly optimistic." Whatever the case, the uncertainty around the XP-67's true capabilities will likely never be definitively settled.

	S-23 4/2/1941[1]	S-23A 5/5/1941[2]	XP-67 AUTHORITY FOR PURCHASE AFP # 182428	XP-67 DEMONSTRATED (PER FINAL REPORT)
Weight empty	13,181lb	13,953lb	(Not covered)	17,745 lb
Normal (design) gross weight	17,056lb	18,600lb	(Not covered)	22,114 lb
High speed @ 35,000ft, Military power	512mph	500mph[3]	(Not covered)	(No data)
High speed @ 25,000ft, Military power	(Not covered)	472mph	462mph	405 MPH[4]
High speed @ 10,000ft(4)	(Not covered)	(Not covered)	(Not covered)	357 MPH[5]
High speed @ 5,000ft, Military power	395mph	384mph	(Not covered)	(No data)
Endurance @ Normal power, any altitude	1 hr[6]	1.0 hr[7]	(Not covered)	(No data)
Time to climb to 25,000ft, Military power 5 min, then Normal	9.0 min	9.0 min	12 min	(No data)
Landing distance over 50ft obstacle	1,689ft	1,700ft	(Not covered)	1,583 ft
Takeoff over 50ft obstacle, sod runway, high lift devices	2,853ft	2,700ft	(Not covered)	3,018 ft[8]
Range @ most economical speed	2,400 mi[9]	2,400 mi[10]	(Not covered)	2,385 mi
Average speed for best range @ 35,000ft	314mph	316mph	(Not covered)	(No data)
Service ceiling	(Not covered)	(Not covered)	41,500ft	(No data)

Very little official flight performance data was taken with the XP-67, making it hard to determine how close it was capable of coming to its contractual requirements. A substantial weight gain, coupled with no increase in horsepower, makes it likely that there would have been significant deficiencies.

(1) Design altitude: 35,000ft (with 5,000ft ram).
(2) Based on specific fuel consumption of 0.65lb/BHP-hr; handwritten note "inconsistent with Military power guarantees."
(3) 1,700bhp per engine at 27,000ft with GE Type D-2 turbosupercharger, plus 6,000ft of ram = 80 percent ram efficiency, giving 1,700bhp at 33,000ft, 1,600bhp at 35,000ft.
(4) 1,600bhp per engine.
(5) 2,100bhp per engine.
(6) 184 gal fuel.
(7) 282 gal fuel.
(8) Not believed to have been on sod, but not actually documented.
(9) Overload fuel.
(10) At 0.48 specific fuel consumption with 740 gal fuel.

XP-67 Variants

Even before the XP-67 took to the air, variants for different roles and missions were being discussed. In fact, its Model 2 precursor had not been submitted to the USAAF for consideration before MAC was using its design as a jumping-off point for at least one highly original concept, the "McDonnell 5 Purpose Pursuit Attack Bomber," officially the Model 2E. A drawing has survived, and it shows that the concept manages to pack not only the typical fighter armament of .50cal and 20mm guns for all five variants, but room was somehow found for 60 fragmentation bombs, or 12 x 100lb demolition bombs, or a single 1,100lb demolition bomb, not to mention a rear gunner position behind the bomb-bay, all while keeping the basic dimensions of the Model 2. A significant difference was the use of Allison V-1710 engines from the outset, since the R40-A selection process was still ongoing and Continental's I-1430 was not yet a player.

A more realistic option surfaced during a phone conversation between Brig Gen Carroll and McDonnell on December 18, 1943, after the first prototype XP-67 had completed its 689 inspection and taxi tests, and was being readied for its first flight. McDonnell, ever alert for new opportunities, had heard through his contacts that the USAAF had an urgent need for long-range reconnaissance aircraft. His message to Carroll was that by taking out the armament (assuming that the XP-67 ultimately became the P-67) "and a few other things," the aircraft would have a range of about 4,000 miles and an average speed (a term that must have depended heavily on an unspecified list of assumptions) of 325mph. Carroll confirmed that "they" wanted a

Boasting an official MAC drawing number, the 5 Purpose Pursuit Attack Bomber gives a glimpse into the creativity and ingenuity of the MAC design staff in the very early pre-contract days. (Ron Farver Collection)

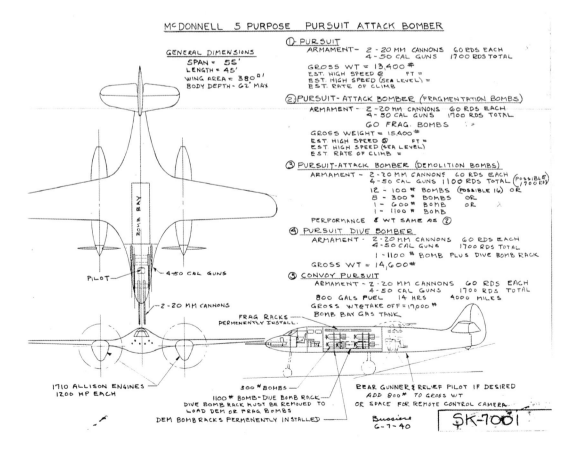

long-range airplane all right, but immediately asked whether MAC could put two people in it; in fact, he said "they" wanted three, but could make do with two. McDonnell said that it would be possible to add a seat behind the pilot, in the space between the front and rear wing spars, and even claimed that "we could put three in just as well as two if we were changing it." He then revealed that MAC had already done a study for a reconnaissance aircraft, but had left it as a single-seater. Adding another one or two crew, he said, would be a major change that would decrease the range from the 4,000-mile estimate. The best location for the cameras was not in the nose, like the F-5 variant of the P-38, probably because most of that volume was unavoidably taken up by the nose landing gear bay. Instead, they were to be mounted behind the rear wing spar. When Carroll asked whether that would impact the fuel quantity, a major advantage of the XP-67's extreme blending was revealed by McDonnell: "Those wings are so thick thru the center section we can still get in addition to that something on the order of 1100 gallons of gas, maybe 1200. With that extra man the range would probably be cut down from 4000 miles to probably about 3500." Carroll proposed that MAC do a "little preliminary study" on fitting in a second man, to which a clearly disappointed McDonnell replied, "You feel sure there would be no interest with one man?" Carroll responded with a very interesting point: "That is why they are not satisfied with the P-38; they have the range but they want two people." McDonnell agreed to do the study, but nothing more is known about it.

The one-man reconnaissance variant, however, was unofficially designated P-67E (McDonnel Model 16A) and drawings of it have survived, apparently showing exactly the layout that had been described to Brig Gen Carroll. Among the things revealed by the drawings is the replacement of the heavily framed canopy with a bubble design that would give much better all-around visibility, although careful scrutiny of the three-view reveals a significant difference in its location on the side and top views, for unknown reasons. The raised horizontal tail and enlarged vertical tail are in evidence as well, along with the mixed piston/jet powerplant that was clearly going to be needed in the absence of I-1430 production. The General Arrangement drawing calls out the Packard-build Merlin for the piston engine, while the Inboard Profile keeps the Allison option open. A drop tank is shown mounted asymmetrically below the center fuselage, to help boost range for the mission. The top view shows that the "3-C" leading edge was very much in evidence here.

In August 1944, the USAAF's interest in this variant was formalized in a letter signed by Brig Gen Marvin Gross stating that: "[t]he Reconnaissance Branch, Requirements Division, is interested in the P-67 (Conversion E) for use as a long range photographic airplane to replace the F-5 and possibly the F-6 . . . The expected performance data, submitted by the McDonnell Aircraft Corporation, provides the following advantages over present types: a. Practical photographic range – 3,149 miles. b. High speed at 32,000 feet – 569 miles per hour. c. High speed at sea level – 511 miles per hour. d. Service ceiling – 49,700 feet. e. Vibration free photography by operating on jet engines only."

Opposite
The Inboard Profile shows internal details of the P-67E's mixed propulsion system in each nacelle. The XP-67's wing leading edge inlets have been retained, but now provide air for the I-20 jet engine in each nacelle. The inboard wing sections that were reserved for armament on the XP-67 have been converted into large self-sealing fuel tanks to replace the fuel volume lost when the aft fuselage was turned into a photo equipment bay for single vertical and twin oblique cameras, with associated flat panel windows. The inclusion of section cuts is rare on surviving drawings, making this an even more significant piece of history. (Greater St Louis Air and Space Museum)

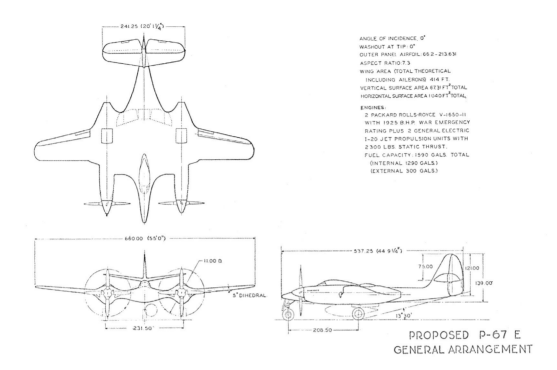

ANGLE OF INCIDENCE. 0°
WASHOUT AT TIP: 0°
OUTER PANEL AIRFOIL: 66.2 - 213.631
ASPECT RATIO 7.3
WING AREA (TOTAL THEORETICAL
    INCLUDING AILERONS) 414 FT.
VERTICAL SURFACE AREA 67.31 FT² TOTAL
HORIZONTAL SURFACE AREA 104.0 FT² TOTAL

ENGINES:
    2 PACKARD ROLLS-ROYCE V-1650-11
    WITH 1925 B.H.P. WAR EMERGENCY
    RATING PLUS 2 GENERAL ELECTRIC
    I-20 JET PROPULSION UNITS WITH
    2300 LBS. STATIC THRUST.
    FUEL CAPACITY: 1590 GALS. TOTAL
        (INTERNAL 1290 GALS.)
        (EXTERNAL 300 GALS.)

PROPOSED P-67 E
GENERAL ARRANGEMENT

The proposed P-67E presents a clean, modern appearance at the end of the piston-engine fighter era. The 300-gallon drop tank is mounted asymmetrically below the center fuselage, to help boost range for the reconnaissance mission. (Greater St Louis Air and Space Museum)

There were disadvantages listed, too, including the lack of a pressurized cockpit, inability to mount long focal length (40in.) cameras for high altitude photography, no provisions for low altitude forward oblique photography for tactical reconnaissance, and most telling of all, "the engine nacelles are cutting off well over 50 per cent of the horizon on the oblique photographs of the tri-metrogon camera installation."

Misinformation was running rampant at the time, due to a lack of released information on the classified XP-67 program, leading to the belief expressed in this letter that "one (1) P-67 (Conversion D) is now flying and . . . the McDonnell Aircraft Corporation intends to produce another P-67 (Conversion E) in the near future." After outlining a few requests for changes, Brig Gen Gross concludes with "[r]equest that this office be informed as to practicability of above in P-67 (Conversion E) of this

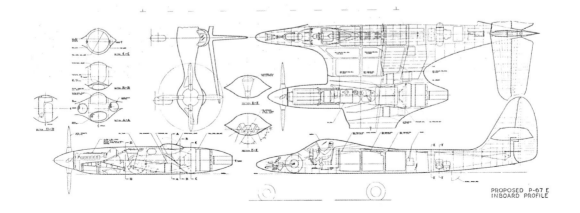

PROPOSED P-67 E
INBOARD PROFILE

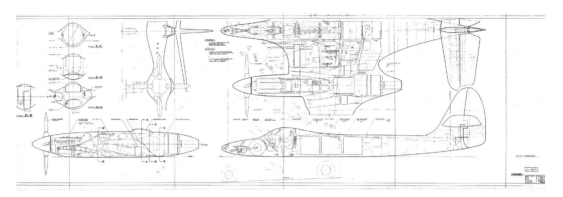

McDonnell aircraft and also the approximate date No. 1 model of same can be produced." It would be interesting to know how MAC responded to this, but such a response does not seem to have survived. The "Conversion D" referred to in the letter corresponds to McDonnell Model 16, but again, no existing documentation has been found, although it seems highly likely that it was very similar to what MAC called the "XP-67C."

A fighter version was also drawn at about the same time, sharing an identical outline with the P-67E but differing substantially beneath the skin. Designated on its Inboard Profile as the "XP-67 Conversion C" and also the "XP-67C," it restores the fuselage fuel tankage and armament that the P-67E had usurped, and deletes the cameras and their flat panel windows. It seems to have been assigned the unwieldy McDonnell Model Number 12F32-120-S-C, "Long Range, Pursuit, Twin Engine (Model F32-120-S) Conversion 'C'."

As mentioned earlier, an attack variant was also discussed. McDonnell raised the possibility during a visit to Materiel Command at Wright Field on December 19, 1942. The Engineering Division felt that the XP-67 would be unsuitable for the mission, but thought that it might be better able to meet the requirements for "support type airplanes." As the Case History report summarizes it from the January 1, 1943, letter by Brig Gen Carroll to McDonnell, "since no further development of this type of airplane was necessary, the present XP-67 program was not going to be changed." This was eventually proven true, after D-Day the next year, when existing tactical aircraft were turned over to the ground attack role with great success.

Trying to maintain interest in a faltering program, MAC prepared a marketing package called "Confidential Engineering Report No. 236" that shows what might have been, had things gone better with the XP-67. It describes fighter, fighter-bomber, and photographic reconnaissance versions, as variants under the general P-67C descriptor. The presented configuration featured two Packard Merlin V-1650-11 engines with two-stage, two-speed, engine-driven superchargers yielding 1,825bhp, augmented by two General Electric I-20 jet engines, each having 2,300lb static thrust, both numbers being at War Emergency rating at sea level.

Provisions were made for four external stations capable of carrying either bombs or expendable fuel tanks. A variety of attack and reconnaissance missions were presented, with truly amazing performance possibilities. Speeds in the baseline fighter configuration were estimated as 502mph

The P-67C fighter variant. Although this is a genuine MAC drawing, for some reason the top view and front view show different arrangements of armament. The text in that region gives three options: 12 x .50cal machine guns (total 4,800 rounds), 8 x 20mm T-26 cannon (total 2,208 rounds), or 4 x 37mm M10 cannon with unspecified number of rounds. The top view shows the last option, while the front view shows an XP-67 type arrangement of three guns per side, presumably also 37mm M10s. Why the outboard one on each side was omitted from the drawing but included in the note is a mystery. (Gerald Balzer, Greater St Louis Air and Space Museum)

DIMENSIONS	XP-67 (MAC DRAWING SK-346, APR 1943)	XP-67 MARCH 1944 REWORK	XP-67 AUGUST 1944 REWORK	P-67C	P-67E
Length	44ft 9¾in.	(No data)	(No data)	44ft 9¼in.	44ft 9¼in.
Wingspan	55ft 1⅜in.	55ft	55ft	55ft	55ft
Height, from ground	14ft 9in.	15ft 9in.	15ft 9in.	(No data)	(No data)
Height, from bottom of fuselage (datum line)	9ft 1in.	10ft 1in.	10ft 1in.	11ft 7in.	11ft 7in.
Wing area (including ailerons)	414 sqft	414 sqft	414 sqft	414 sqft	414 sqft
Wing aspect ratio	7.3	7.3	7.3	7.3	7.3
Wing dihedral	5°	5°	7°	5°	5°
Wing taper ratio	2.37:1	2.37:1	2.37:1	(No data)	(No data)
Wing mean aerodynamic chord (MAC)	8ft 4in.	8ft 4in.	8ft 4in.	(No data)	(No data)
Wing airfoil	NACA 66,2-213.6	NACA 66,2-213.6	NACA 66,2-213.6	NACA 66,2-213.6	NACA 66,2-213.631
Horizontal tail span	20ft 4in.	20ft 4in.	20ft 4in.	20ft 1¼in.	20ft 1¼in.
Horizontal tail dihedral	8°36'34"	8°36'34"	8°36'34"	(No data)	(No data)
Horizontal tail surface area	103.6 sqft	103.6 sqft	103.6 sqft	104.0 sqft	104.0 sqft
Vertical [tail] surface area	58.23 sqft	58.23 sqft	58.23 sqft	67.31 sqft	67.31 sqft
Nacelle separation	18ft 4in.	18ft 4in.	18ft 4in.	(No data)	(No data)
Maximum ground angle	12°30'	12°30'	12°30'	13°30'	13°30'
Wheel base	15ft 8½in.	15ft 8½in.	15ft 8½in.	17ft 4½in.	17ft 4½in.
Wheel track	17ft 9½in.	(No data)	(No data)	19ft 3½in.	19ft 3½in.
Propeller diameter	10ft 6in.[1]	10ft 6in.[1]	10ft 6in.[1]	11ft	11ft
Propeller gear ratio	1:2.277	(No data)	(No data)	(No data)	(No data)
Flap deflection angle	45°[2]	(No data)	(No data)	(No data)	(No data)

It was anticipated that any performance deficiencies found in the XP-67 flight testing would be more than overcome by adding jet engines in the nacelles for production versions P-67C (fighter) and P-67E (photo-reconnaissance.)

(1) The XP-67 Final Report shows 10ft 8in. but all other sources show 10ft 6in., so this is believed to be a typo.

(2) Taken from January-March 1942 drawing 2-00000 "General Arrangement Interceptor-Pursuit."

at sea level, 560mph at 18,500ft, and 559mph at 32,000ft. This would actually have made the P-67C/E faster than Lockheed's contemporary P-80 at altitude, and with vastly longer range and endurance, since estimates showed a combat radius of 780 miles with internal armament and an external fuel tank, or 615 miles with three 1,000lb bombs. The P-67E would have had a "photographic range" of 2,707 miles with one 300-gallon and one 150-gallon external tank. These kinds of ranges would have been very useful in the Pacific Theater, dominated by huge areas of water between home bases and targets.

In February 1944, an unusual request was made to the chief of the Aircraft Laboratory at Wright Field by Col Bogert, stemming from a telephone conversation with a Mr. Dunham at the Aircraft Lab. As a result of that conversation, Bogert was requesting a performance study of the XP-67 fitted with a compounded V-1430 engine, and his memo says that "[e]ngine specification, installation drawings and other information have been furnished to your Laboratory by Mr. Snyder of Continental." Such a concept had been raised in a letter from Col J. F. Phillips, Chief of Development Engineering Branch, Materiel Division, Washington, DC, to Col J. M. Gillespie, Chief of the Powerplant Lab, Materiel Command at Wright Field, which described equipping the I-1430 with "a turbo supercharger for transmission of power back to the crankshaft . . . Such a development appeared worthy of consideration in view of the apparently energetic engineering staff at Continental."

Continental engineers actually worked with their General Electric (GE) counterparts on this study, which is logical since GE was in the forefront of technology development on gas turbines at this time. The chief obstacle to compounding was the scarcity of materials for the turbine that could stand up to direct impingement to high-temperature engine exhaust gases, and GE certainly had up-to-date experience with that, thanks to its work on jet turbine engines. At a follow-up conference in January 1944, layout drawings of a compounded I-1430 engine in the XP-67 were presented, along with estimated performance. For each engine option (compounded I-1430 and normal I-1430 with conventional turbo-supercharger), the same useful load was carried. The compounded engines added only 60lb to the weight of the aircraft, and the effect on performance was intriguing. According to the meeting notes, "There is a substantial over-all improvement in performance without compromising the design when incorporating the compound engine installation . . . The maximum range is increased approximately 25 percent using the compound engine due to the lower specific fuel consumption." It was recommended that development of the concept be expedited "since all phases of the [XP-67] aircraft performance indicated decided improvement."

But nothing was to come of this. Like so many other promising ideas, changing priorities as the jet age was dawning meant that piston-engine concepts took a decided back seat. Turbojets and turboprops were able to offer equivalent power without the mechanical complexities of a piston engine up front, and their deficiencies in range and acceleration relative to propeller-driven aircraft would rapidly be reduced as their technologies matured.

From beginning to end, then, the XP-67's family tree shows much innovation and fresh thinking.

In the end, the XP-67 remained as it had begun, a tantalizing concept of unproven benefit. It was years in the making, moments in the undoing. But the program did have payoffs, some of its key features being adapted to other, more successful, aircraft.

The XP-67 grew out of Martin's twin-engine bombers, and ultimately touched the jet age with mixed-propulsion variants P-67C and E. Drawings are not to scale. (National Archives; Ron Farver Collection; Gerald Balzer Collection, Greater St Louis Air and Space Museum)

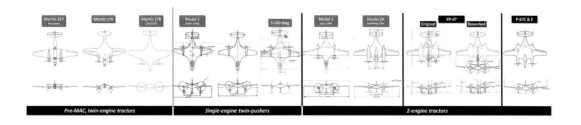

CHAPTER FOUR

INFLUENCE ON FRONTLINE TYPES

The XP-67 may not have gone into production; neither did any of the other winners of X-plane contracts under R40-C, or, for that matter, any of the advanced engines selected from R40-A. But it did have two lasting effects on future aircraft in general, and MAC fighters in particular.

First, before the XP-67 there had been no database for designers to draw on concerning its unusual style of inlet ducts carved out of a wing leading edge. In the Model 1 and 2 stages of its development, this caused a good deal of head-scratching at NACA, judging by contemporary citations. Similarly, there was little data on the aerodynamics and control issues inherent in highly blended wing/nacelle/fuselage airframes. XP-67 data thus became a foundation on which future design teams could build.

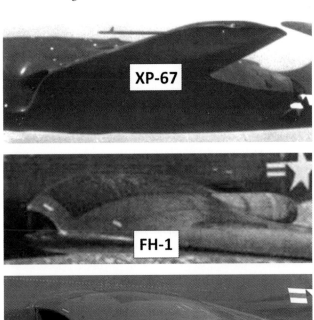

Wing/nacelle blending lessons from the XP-67 led the way to McDonnell's first two generations of jet fighters, the Phantom I and Banshee. (Greater St Louis Air and Space Museum, Gerald Balzer Collection)

Second, MAC itself benefitted from the XP-67 not solely because of that data, but because of the experience that it gave the company's fledgling team in understanding how to plan, estimate, and execute a complex Government aircraft program. Even the most seasoned of MAC's core group of engineers who had come with McDonnell from Glenn L. Martin lacked experience in high-performance fighters; they had been working on medium bombers and large seaplanes. The XP-67 developed MAC expertise in a whole new area, and set the stage for an amazing run of successes, which over the next few decades would see the company become the largest manufacturer of fighter aircraft in the Free World.

Some of those aircraft would show definite linkages to the unique features of the XP-67. MAC's first jet fighter, the XFD-1 (later FH-1 Phantom), designed under US Navy contract during the same period that the XP-67 was having its struggles, incorporated smooth blending of its twin jet engines with the wings and fuselage. Its engines were mounted in the fuselage/wing interface rather than in nacelles like the XP-67's, but with blending the design looked much sleeker than Bell's contemporary P-59. Despite the fact that the P-59 (a larger, heavier aircraft, but with more powerful engines) had a thrust-to-weight ratio of 0.36, while the FH-1's was just 0.32, the MAC fighter was 80 knots faster, thanks to its cleaner, lower drag configuration.

The FH-1 saw limited service and was quickly supplanted by the next MAC product, the F2H Banshee. The same proven blending was refined to fit this more advanced fighter, and the result was a machine that gave MAC its first of what would one day become an avalanche of international orders.

Much later, a peculiar concept called Quiet Attack appeared at McDonnell Douglas, and in an age dominated by angular wings and minimal fillets, its smooth curvatures were reminiscent of what the XP-67 was trying to achieve. It never proceeded beyond drawings, but it heralded a subtle change in military aircraft design in general.

The XP-67's features can thus be traced through a whole series of subsequent MAC designs. As usual in such pioneering cases, later developments become more refined and gradually take on their own unique identities, but the influence is always traceable.

Extreme blending turned out to have unforeseen advantages in areas other than aerodynamics. Decades later, the B-1 and B-2 bombers would emerge with highly faired engines and wings as a key part of their low observability or "stealth" properties.

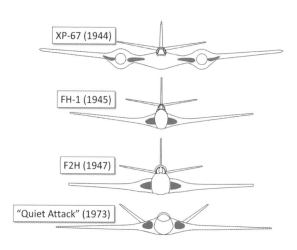

From USAAC beginnings to US Navy applications. (Authors' drawings)

Highly blended techniques pioneered by the XP-67 have made a comeback, and aircraft using them are still flying today. (US Government source)

CONCLUSION

The XP-67 had a difficult life. Its original ancestor, the Model 1, was rejected by its intended customer, even though four different variants had been proposed. James McDonnell was determined to land a contract, though, and so the redesigned Model 2 was born. It too failed. Yet McDonnell persevered with a concept that he and his engineers believed in, with the refined Model 2A. At last, he had a winner, and the XP-67 was a straightforward development of Model 2A, but the contract that was awarded on September 30, 1941, did not produce a flying prototype until January 6, 1944, well over two years later. There were many excellent reasons for this, and in today's world that would be a phenomenally quick timeline to achieve. Yet at the time, others were much quicker to the punch. North American Aviation brought into being the NA-73 aircraft (that would become the legendary P-51 Mustang) in just under six months; Lockheed had the P-80 jet fighter ready in almost exactly that same time. It is often argued that MAC's effort was protracted because it used a temperamental experimental engine, while the NA-73 used the tried and proven Allison, but as we have seen, the I-1430's reputation for problems was mostly a myth. In any case, the P-80 used not just a new experimental engine, but an entirely new kind of engine, and still got into the air in much less time than McDonnell's first fighter.

Had the XP-67 been able to even approximately match the timelines of these other American fighters, its future might have gone much more smoothly. The USAAC wanted it as the aircraft answered unique operational needs, and the specifications that were drawn up to guide its development were based on a perception of reality as it existed before the attack on Pearl Harbor. By the time the XP-67 was finally ready for its performance demonstration runs in September 1944, Allied forces were advancing on the ground toward Germany and closing an ever-shrinking ring around Japan. It had become a vastly different world, with vastly different mission needs. The "Flying Fillet" had become largely irrelevant in a world where tens of thousands of aircraft were already filling virtually every conceivable mission niche. Its legacy, rather than a sterling record of combat achievements, would be the far less visible, but no less important, pioneering role that produced data to guide future designers.

BIBLIOGRAPHY

The basics of the XP-67 program, and in particular its unique engine, have been covered by many authors over the years. Placing the program in context with other X-planes and operational aircraft was beyond the scope of this book, but the following can be used as supplements in those areas. They also give more complete descriptions of programmatic elements relating to how the McDonnell Aircraft Corporation interacted with the USAAC immediately after the company's formation, when the XP-67 was being conceived and developed, which could easily fill an entire book by itself.

BOOKS

Balzer, Gerald H., *American Secret Pusher Fighters of World War II*, Specialty Press, North Branch, MN (2008)

Buttler, Tony and Griffith, Alan, *American Secret Projects: Fighters, Bombers and Attack Aircraft 1937–1945*, Crecy Publishing, Manchester, UK (2015)

Norton, Bill, *U.S. Experimental & Prototype Aircraft Projects, Fighters 1939–1945,* Specialty Press, North Branch, MN (2008)

DOCUMENTS

AAF Technical Report 5412, *Final Report on the XP-67 Airplane*, Army Air Forces Air Materiel Command, Wright Field, Dayton, OH (January 31, 1946)

Case History of XP-67 Airplane, Historical Division, Intelligence, T-2, Air Materiel Command, Wright Field, Dayton, OH (July 23, 1946)

Green, Thomas H., *The Development of Air Doctrine in the Army Air Arm 1917–1941*, Office of Air Force History, Washington, DC (September 1955)

McDonnell Aircraft Corporation, *Confidential Engineering Report No. 236* (P-67C) (undated)

McDonnell Aircraft Corporation Report No. 42 Addenda 3, *Analysis of Wind Tunnel Data ⅛ Scale Model Addenda III* (March 13, 1942)

NACA Memorandum Report MR No. L4J28, *Drag Measurements at High Reynolds Numbers of Two Practical-Construction NACA 66,2-214 (Approx.) Wing Sections for the McDonnell XP-67 Airplane*, Langley Memorial Aeronautical Laboratory, Langley Field, VA (undated)

NACA Memorandum Report (unnumbered), *Spin Tests of a 1/27-Scale Model of the McDonnell XP-67 Airplane*, Langley Memorial Aeronautical Laboratory, Langley Field, VA (August 29, 1942)

NACA Research Memorandum RM No. L7E15, *Compilation of Test Data on 111 Free-Spinning Airplane Models Tested in the Langley 15-Foot and 20-Foot Free-Spinning Tunnels*, Langley Memorial Aeronautical Laboratory, Langley Field, VA (undated)

NACA Research Memorandum (unnumbered), *Wind-Tunnel Investigation of the Aerodynamic Characteristics of a ¼–scale model of the McDonnell XP-67 Airplane*, Langley Memorial Aeronautical Laboratory, Langley Field, VA (January 31, 1944)

WEB RESOURCES

https://www.afhra.af.mil/
http://www.enginehistory.org/ (Aircraft Engine Historical Society site)
https://oldmachinepress.com/
http://rwebs.net/avhistory/opsman/geturbo/geturbo.htm
https://thereaderwiki.com/en/Continental_IV-1430

INDEX